Delectable Collectables

Chester County Historical Society

CHESTER COUNTY HISTORICAL SOCIETY

Library of Congress Catalog Number: 00-133334
ISBN: 0-929706-15-3
Edited, Designed and Manufactured by
Favorite Recipes® Press
an imprint of

FRP

P.O. Box 305142, Nashville, Tennessee 37230
800-358-0560

Manufactured in the United States of America
First Printing: Millennium 2000 Edition   10,000 copies

This cookbook is a collection of favorite recipes, which are not necessarily original recipes.

INTRODUCTION

The idea of a cookbook is not a new one for the Chester County Historical Society. In fact many of the recipes in this collection are from a file collected several years ago by the CCHS' volunteers. True to our mission, we collect and save everything worthwhile. However, it took a group of dedicated, talented and determined cooks and history buffs to turn dreams into reality. And what a group it is! The Recipe Committee has solicited recipes from some of Chester Country's best cooks and chefs. They have tested them not so much for ingredients and taste, delicious flavor being a foregone conclusion, but for accurate measurements. The Editorial Committee has researched and uncovered exciting and interesting historical facts and the Design Committee has determined the aesthetic quality of the publication. They have produced not only a fabulous collection of delicious recipes but also some insight to Chester County's past and the institution that strives to promote an understanding of its history by collecting, preserving, exhibiting and interpreting it and its relationship to the region for audiences of all ages and interests.

CCHS was founded in 1893 as a small repository for manuscript and library material by a group of civic-minded residents whose goal was to satisfy intellectual curiosity, diffuse knowledge and cultivate patriotism as well as regional and national pride. Today, CCHS has grown into a multi-purposed educational and cultural institution that serves tens of thousands of people per year.

Behind all of these programs are people who love Chester County and its history, the CCHS members, the expert staff and especially the devoted, selfless volunteers who share so much time, energy and knowledge. We invite you to enjoy this latest volunteer effort and thank you for participating by purchasing our book. The proceeds we realize from this project will be invested in our educational programs.

Sally Graham
Sandy Manthorpe
Co-editors

DEDICATION

We dedicate this book with heartfelt thanks

and deep gratitude to all who volunteer for the

Chester County Historical Society.

With their talents and commitment,

CCHS will continue to preserve the past

and be a beacon to the future.

CHESTER COUNTY HISTORICAL SOCIETY

ACKNOWLEDGEMENTS

CO-EDITORS, COOKBOOK COMMITTEE
Sally Graham and Sandy Manthorpe

RECIPE COMMITTEE

Co-Chairs
Linda-Lee Egen
Barbara Jo Spellman

Joanne Alegado
Terry Anstey
George Graham III
Diane Frame
Andrea Glidden
Doris Hemker
Sandy Kalemjian
Wynne Milner
Pam Smith
Diane Stevens

Tea suggestions by
Sam H. G. Twining, L.V.O.
—R. Twining and Company Limited

MARKETING COMMITTEE

Co-Chairs
Phyllis Copeland
Sally Graham

Joanne Alegado
Teresa Ciccotelli
Patrick Comerford
Anne Congdon
Dave Davis
Gay Denny
Roger Grigson
Jean Hoover
Ann Kampf
Alison Mallamo
Mary Elizabeth Pomeroy
Andrea Sankaran
Susan Schultz

ARTWORK AND DESIGN COMMITTEE

Chair
Nancy Thompson

Ellen Endslow
Rob Lukens
Sandy Manthorpe
Carol Thompson
Nancy Pike
Hope Wood
Ellen Vander Noot

DESIGN AND PHOTOGRAPHY

Photographer
George Fistrovich

Icon and line art
Nancy Thompson

EDITORIAL COMMITTEE

Jane Brosius
Carol Grigson
Kathy Head

Chair
Karen Helm

Diane Rofini
Wesley Sollenberger
Marion Strode

Front cover painting, "Old Horticultural Hall" by Barclay Rubincam (1920–1978).
From the Chester County Historical Society collection. Barclay Rubincam was a native of
Chester County, born in Greer Valley near Unionville. He was a full-time artist who specialized in
landscapes, portraits and still life painting. He was a close friend of Andrew Wyeth and studied
under N. C. Wyeth, Frank Schoonover and Gail Hoskins. His paintings portray the nostalgic
agrarian life and landmarks along the historic Brandywine.

Back cover painting, "Mr. Stewart's Cheshire Hounds" by F. B. Voss, 1948.
From the collection of Mrs. John B. Hannum, MFH.

NUTRITIONAL GUIDELINES

The editors have attempted to present these recipes in a format that allows approximate nutritional values to be computed. Persons with dietary or health problems or whose diets require close monitoring should not rely solely on the nutritional information provided. They should consult their physician or a registered dietitian for specific information.

Abbreviations for Nutritional Profile

Cal – Calories	T Fat – Total Fat	Sod – Sodium
Prot – Protein	Chol – Cholesterol	g – grams
Carbo – Carbohydrates	Fiber – Dietary Fiber	mg – milligrams

Nutritional information for these recipes is computed from information derived from many sources, including materials supplied by the United States Department of Agriculture, computer databanks, and journals in which the information is assumed to be in the public domain. However, many specialty items, new products, and processed food may not be available from these sources or may vary from the average values used in these profiles. More information on new and/or specific products may be obtained by reading the nutrient labels.

Unless otherwise specified, the nutritional profile of these recipes is based on all measurements being level.

- Artificial sweeteners vary in use and strength so should be used "to taste," using the recipe ingredients as a guideline. Sweeteners using aspartame (NutraSweet and Equal) should not be used as a sweetener in recipes involving prolonged heating, which reduces the sweet taste. For further information on the use of these sweeteners, refer to the package.
- Alcoholic ingredients have been analyzed for the basic information. Cooking causes the evaporation of alcohol, which decreases alcoholic and caloric content.
- Buttermilk, sour cream, and yogurt are the types available commercially.
- Cake mixes which are prepared using package directions include 3 eggs and 1/2 cup oil.
- Chicken, cooked for boning and chopping, has been roasted, which yields the lowest caloric values.
- Cottage cheese is cream-style with 4.2 percent creaming mixture. Dry curd cottage cheese has no creaming mixture.
- Eggs are all large. To avoid raw eggs that may carry salmonella, as in eggnog or 6-week muffin batter, use an equivalent amount of commercial egg substitute.
- Flour is unsifted all-purpose flour.
- Garnishes, serving suggestions, (or more) ingredients and other optional information and variations are not included in the profile.
- Margarine and butter are regular, not whipped or presoftened.
- Milk is whole milk, 3.5 percent butterfat. Low-fat milk is 1 percent butterfat. Evaporated milk is whole milk with 60 percent of the water removed.
- Oil is any type of vegetable cooking oil. Shortening is hydrogenated vegetable shortening.
- Salt and other ingredients to taste as noted in the ingredients have not been included in the nutritional profile.
- If a choice of ingredients has been given, the profile reflects the first option. If a choice of amounts has been given, the profile reflects the greater amount.

TABLE OF CONTENTS

*Indicates menu and menu recipes.

"WHERE WILL ALL THESE HISTORICAL TREASURES BE STORED?"

The Chester County Historical Society was founded in 1893 by a group of civic-minded West Chester residents. Their concern for the preservation of county archives led them to establish a small repository for manuscript and library materials in Library Hall in West Chester. Within two years, after amassing a sizeable collection of books, pamphlets, magazines, and newspapers, *The Daily Local News* ran an editorial asking "Where will all these historical treasures be stored?" The answer to that question has been an evolving one.

First, the State Normal School provided a large room in its new library for the Society. While its collection of archives grew rapidly, the Society also began a series of activities to educate the public about the county's colorful and important history. By 1937 CCHS was ready to move into its third home, Horticultural Hall. Designed in 1848 by Thomas U. Walter, a Philadelphia architect, Horticultural Hall had enjoyed its own rich history of ownership and, by 1937, it was known as Memorial Hall. Shortly after the building was dedicated by its new owners in 1942, the Historical Society hired its first full-time professional staff.

For the first time, the institution had ample gallery and storage space, and its small collection of decorative arts began to grow. Soon the Historical Society boasted a sizeable and important collection of furniture, needlework, paintings, silver, redware, porcelain, and textiles, which continues to grow to this day. CCHS began to evolve from a regional museum into one which today enjoys a national reputation and significance.

Adaptations to the building in 1970 added more gallery space and, in 1995, The History Center opened in what had been the old YMCA building. Joined by an enclosed bridge, the two buildings present a modern complex where permanent and changing exhibits, a library, office and storage space, a museum shop, and public program space provide a unique opportunity for visitors, researchers, and students of all ages. A dedicated professional staff and a corps of volunteers make the Chester County Historical Society a museum where history comes alive.

Exhibit Opening Reception

**Sesame Eggplant Salsa with
Parmesan Pita Chips**
(PAGE 14)

Broiled Crab Meltaways
(PAGE 25)

Cheese Almond Fingers
(PAGE 24)

Fruit and Cheese

Crudités with Dip

Wyeth Not Clam Pie
(PAGE 19)

Cranberry Tea
(PAGE 125)

Pembroke Punch
(PAGE 31)

Twinings Ceylon Breakfast Tea Iced
(PAGE 30)

ARTICHOKE AND SPINACH DIP

2 (14-ounce) cans artichoke hearts
1/2 (10-ounce) package frozen chopped spinach
1 1/2 cups mayonnaise
1 cup freshly grated Parmesan cheese
1/4 teaspoon granulated or powdered garlic, or 1 onion, finely chopped
1/2 teaspoon salt
1/8 teaspoon pepper
1 teaspoon fresh lemon juice

Drain the artichoke hearts. Process the artichokes in a food processor just until chopped. Cook the spinach according to the package directions, drain well and squeeze dry. Combine the chopped artichokes, spinach, mayonnaise, Parmesan cheese, garlic, salt, pepper and lemon juice in a large bowl and mix well. Spoon the mixture into a buttered 1 1/2-quart casserole. Bake at 350 degrees for 35 minutes or until bubbly. Place the casserole in a chafing dish or on a warming plate to keep hot. Serve the dip with sturdy crackers. The dip may be refrigerated, covered, for up to two days before baking, or may be frozen and thawed before baking. Yield: 25 servings.

Approx Per Serving: Cal 129; Prot 3 g; Carbo 3 g; T Fat 12 g; 83% Calories from Fat;
Chol 13 mg; Fiber 1 g; Sod 290 mg

"I knew not which to admire most, the appearance of the country, or the neat plump Quaker and his wife . . . they seemed to be the happiest people on earth, health on their cheeks, contentment on their countenance . . . West Chester is a most delectable spot . . . I found more taste, talent and refinement in West Chester, in proportion of the number of inhabitants, than in any town, without exception, I have visited."
—*Anne Royall* (1769–1854) *The Black Book I*
(Washington, D.C., 1828–1829), p. 321.

*HOAGIE DIP

4 ounces boiled ham
4 ounces bologna
4 ounces Genoa salami
4 ounces pepperoni
4 ounces provolone cheese
4 ounces American cheese
1 medium onion
2 medium tomatoes
$^1/_4$ head lettuce
$^1/_4$ cup Hoagie Oil

Process the ham, bologna, salami, pepperoni, provolone and American cheeses and onion in a food processor until chopped. Chop in small batches if necessary to better control the size of the pieces. Coarsely chop the tomatoes and drain in a colander. Process the tomatoes and lettuce in the food processor until desired size. Combine the chopped meat and cheese mixture with the chopped tomatoes and lettuce in a bowl and mix well. Add the Hoagie Oil and mix well. Chill until serving time. Serve the dip with bread pieces or crackers. Yield: 8 servings.

HOAGIE OIL

$^1/_4$ cup vegetable oil
1 teaspoon oregano
$^1/_2$ teaspoon salt
Black pepper and garlic powder to taste

Combine the vegetable oil, oregano, salt, pepper and garlic powder in a small covered container and shake vigorously. Let stand to marry the flavors.

Approx Per Serving: Cal 365; Prot 17 g; Carbo 5 g; T Fat 32 g; 76% Calories from Fat;
Chol 69 mg; Fiber 1 g; Sod 1359 mg

*PORTOBELLO CAVIAR

1¹/₂ pounds portobello mushrooms
2 tablespoons olive oil
1¹/₂ shallots, minced
Minced garlic to taste
1 tablespoon sherry vinegar
Salt and freshly ground pepper to taste

Trim the mushroom stems. Grind the mushrooms coarsely in a food processor. Heat the olive oil in a large skillet over medium-high heat. Add the shallots and garlic. Sauté for 1 to 2 minutes or just until softened. Add the mushrooms and reduce the heat to medium. Cook for 30 minutes or until almost dry, stirring frequently. Add the vinegar. Cook over high heat until the vinegar evaporates, stirring constantly. Remove from the heat. Season with salt and pepper. Spoon into a serving dish. Garnish with parsley. Serve at room temperature with bread and crackers.
Yield: 16 (2-tablespoon) servings.

Approx Per Serving: Cal 26; Prot 2 g; Carbo 2 g; T Fat 2 g; 50% Calories from Fat;
Chol 0 mg; Fiber 2 g; Sod 5 mg

SURPRISE B.L.T. DIP

1 cup mayonnaise
1 cup sour cream
1 pound bacon, crisp-cooked, crumbled
2 large tomatoes, chopped

Combine the mayonnaise and sour cream in a bowl and blend well. Add the bacon and tomatoes and mix well. Serve at room temperature or chilled with Melba toast. May substitute an equivalent amount of spicy salsa for the chopped tomatoes. Yield: 32 (2-tablespoon) servings.

Approx Per Serving: Cal 95; Prot 2 g; Carbo 1 g; T Fat 9 g; 89% Calories from Fat;
Chol 12 mg; Fiber <1 g; Sod 117 mg

*SESAME EGGPLANT SALSA WITH PARMESAN PITA CRISPS

2 (1- to 1¹/₄-pound) eggplants   ³/₄ cup packed minced green onions
2¹/₂ tablespoons minced peeled fresh gingerroot
4 garlic cloves, minced   1 teaspoon chili-garlic sauce
1 tablespoon vegetable or peanut oil
3 tablespoons light brown sugar   2 tablespoons soy sauce
1 tablespoon rice vinegar
2 teaspoons fresh lemon juice   2 large plum tomatoes
³/₄ cup packed finely chopped cilantro
1¹/₂ teaspoons oriental sesame oil   Salt and pepper to taste
1 tablespoon minced green onion
1 tablespoon minced cilantro   Parmesan Pita Crisps

Pierce the eggplants all over with a fork and place on a baking sheet. Bake at 425 degrees for 1 hour or until very soft, turning frequently. Cool slightly. Cut into halves and scoop the pulp into a strainer; drain for 30 minutes. Pulse the eggplant pulp in a food processor until almost smooth. Sauté ³/₄ cup green onions, gingerroot, garlic and chili-garlic sauce in hot vegetable oil in a large heavy skillet for 45 seconds. Add the brown sugar, soy sauce, rice vinegar and lemon juice and mix well. Bring to a simmer, stirring constantly. Add the eggplant pulp and mix well. Cook for 2 minutes or until heated through. Seed the tomatoes and chop finely. Add the tomatoes, ³/₄ cup cilantro and sesame oil to the skillet and mix well. Cool to room temperature. Season with salt and pepper. Place in a serving bowl and sprinkle with 1 tablespoon minced green onion and 1 tablespoon minced cilantro. Serve with Parmesan Pita Crisps. Yield: 20 servings.

PARMESAN PITA CRISPS

6 (6-inch) pita rounds   6 tablespoons olive oil
1¹/₄ cups freshly grated Parmesan cheese

Split each pita round into 2 rounds. Brush the rounds with olive oil and sprinkle with Parmesan cheese. Cut each round into 6 wedges and arrange in a single layer on baking sheets. Bake at 325 degrees for 12 minutes or until golden brown and crisp. Let stand until cool. May store in airtight containers at room temperature for up to 3 days and reheat at 325 degrees for about 5 minutes.

Approx Per Serving: Cal 151; Prot 5 g; Carbo 17 g; T Fat 7 g; 43% Calories from Fat; Chol 5 mg; Fiber 2 g; Sod 359 mg

ALMOND PÂTÉ

1/2 onion
1 garlic clove
8 ounces fresh mushrooms
1/4 teaspoon salt
1/8 teaspoon tarragon
White pepper to taste
2 tablespoons butter
1 (10-ounce) package blanched whole almonds, toasted
1 tablespoon dry sherry
1 tablespoon heavy cream

Place the onion and garlic in a food processor and pulse until coarsely chopped. Set the onion mixture aside. Place the mushrooms in the food processor and pulse until coarsely chopped. Sauté the onion mixture and mushrooms with the salt, tarragon and pepper in the butter in a skillet until the mixture is almost dry. Set aside to cool. Reserve 2/3 cup of the almonds for garnish. Process the remaining almonds in the food processor until coarsely chopped. Reserve 2 tablespoons of the coarsely chopped almonds. Process the remaining almonds until a smooth paste forms. Add the mushrooms mixture to the processor with the sherry and cream and process until smooth. Add the reserved 2 tablespoons coarsely chopped almonds and mix with a single pulse. Place the mixture in a small bowl. Chill, covered, until almost serving time. Invert the pâté onto a serving plate. Decorate with the reserved 2/3 cup whole almonds to resemble a pine cone. Yield: 8 servings.

Approx Per Serving: Cal 251; Prot 8 g; Carbo 8 g; T Fat 22 g; 75% Calories from Fat;
Chol 10 mg; Fiber 3 g; Sod 107 mg

Rebecca Lukens (1794–1854) took over management of the Brandywine Ironworks in 1813 and built it into a major enterprise which would eventually become the Lukens Steel Co., much to the surprise of her male competitors. She became known as "Woman of Steel."

*AUSTRALIAN CHEESE BALL

1 pound medium Cheddar cheese
4 ounces sharp Cheddar cheese
1/4 cup finely chopped gherkins or pickled onions
1/2 cup chopped walnuts
1/2 cup mayonnaise
1 teaspoon lemon juice
2 teaspoons Worcestershire sauce
8 ounces cream cheese, softened
1 cup chopped fresh parsley

Shred the Cheddar cheese. Combine the shredded cheese, gherkins and walnuts in a bowl and mix well. Add the mayonnaise, lemon juice and Worcestershire sauce and mix well. Shape the mixture into a ball, pressing firmly while shaping. Wrap in plastic wrap and refrigerate until thoroughly chilled or almost ready to serve.

Beat the cream cheese in a bowl until smooth and spreadable. Spread the cream cheese evenly over the cheese ball and roll in the chopped parsley to coat well. Place on a serving plate. Serve with cracker biscuits. This cheese ball is a favorite in Australia at Christmastime and decorated with a sprig of holly on top. Yield: 20 servings.

Approx Per Serving: Cal 215; Prot 8 g; Carbo 2 g; T Fat 20 g; 81% Calories from Fat; Chol 46 mg; Fiber <1 g; Sod 266 mg

 How to shine brass (mid-1800s). "The best method for cleaning brass is to pour ammonia over the article to be cleaned and then scrub it thoroughly with the scrubbing brush. In a few minutes the brass will be as bright as new metal. Then rinse in clean water and wipe very dry."

BOURSIN CHEESE

8 ounces cream cheese, softened
1/4 cup butter, softened
1/2 teaspoon Beau Monde seasoning
1 medium to large garlic clove, pressed
1/4 teaspoon Herbs of Provence
1 teaspoon minced fresh or dried parsley
1 teaspoon water
1/4 teaspoon red wine vinegar
1/4 teaspoon Worcestershire sauce

Combine the cream cheese and butter in a mixing bowl and beat at high speed until the mixture is light and fluffy. Add the Beau Monde seasoning, garlic, Herbs of Provence, parsley, water, vinegar and Worcestershire sauce and beat until well mixed. Pack the mixture into crocks or other containers. Cover tightly and let mellow for 12 hours or longer in the refrigerator. The cheese may be refrigerated for up to 1 month. Yield: 20 servings.

Approx Per Serving: Cal 60; Prot 1 g; Carbo <1 g; T Fat 6 g; 92% Calories from Fat;
Chol 19 mg; Fiber 0 g; Sod 73 mg

HERBS OF PROVENCE

3 tablespoons dried marjoram
3 tablespoons dried thyme
3 tablespoons dried summer savory
1 tablespoon dried sweet basil
1 1/2 teaspoons dried rosemary, crumbled
1/2 teaspoon crushed dried sage
1/2 teaspoon fennel seeds

Combine the marjoram, thyme, summer savory, sweet basil, rosemary, sage and fennel seeds in a small airtight container, seal tightly and shake vigorously until well mixed. Store the unused herb mixture in the container in a cool dry place.

*CHEESE SPREAD

1 pound Velveeta cheese
$^1/_2$ cup mayonnaise
1 (5-ounce) jar horseradish

Cut the cheese into pieces and place in a 4-cup glass measuring cup. Microwave until the cheese melts, stirring frequently. Mix until the cheese is smooth and creamy. Add the mayonnaise and horseradish and mix well. Store the cheese spread in a covered container in the refrigerator. Serve as a spread on crackers, pretzel sticks or bread sticks or heat to use as a sauce on cooked cauliflower or baked potatoes. Yield: 20 servings.

Approx Per Serving: Cal 125; Prot 5 g; Carbo 3 g; T Fat 10 g; 74% Calories from Fat;
Chol 23 mg; Fiber <1 g; Sod 367 mg

 When Joseph Pennock built his home in West Marlborough Township in 1714 he never locked his door so Native people were free to seek shelter whenever they pleased. . . . a custom he continued for the rest of his life.

The Great Minquas Trail, an old Indian trail, extended from Washington Boro on the Susquehanna River in Lancaster County through Chester County to the Philadelphia-Chester area. Beaver skins were transported on this trail, laying the foundation for the county's early commercial development. Part of the trail which ran past West Chester was converted into a major transportation route, now called High Street.

*WEYTH NOT CLAM PIE

2 (8-ounce) cans minced clams
1 medium onion
4 sprigs of parsley
3/4 cup butter
1 teaspoon dried oregano
3/4 cup Italian-style bread crumbs
2 (1-ounce) slices mozzarella cheese

Place the clams in a bowl. Chop the onion and parsley finely and add to the bowl. Melt the butter and add to the bowl, mixing well. Crush the oregano and add to the clam mixture with the bread crumbs. Stir until the mixture is well mixed. Spoon into an 8-inch pie plate. Cut the cheese slices into 1-inch strips and arrange decoratively over the clam mixture. Bake at 325 degrees for 20 minutes. May prepare ahead and bake just before serving. Serve with crackers. Yield: 10 servings.

Approx Per Serving: Cal 211; Prot 9 g; Carbo 8 g; T Fat 16 g; 68% Calories from Fat;
Chol 58 mg; Fiber 1 g; Sod 364 mg

Chester County scrapple or Strode's Scrapple. Strode's scrapple was established in 1875 by Amos Darlington Strode. The scrapple business ran for 110 years. "Strode's went back so far that it carried one of the earliest USDA inspection numbers—71." In 1893 the company opened a stand at the Reading Terminal Market [Philadelphia, Pa.] being, "one of the earliest tenants of the market." Strode was the only scrapple maker to put some of its product up in tin cans. The scrapple was shipped across the country to, "the tables of San Francisco, . . . elite cafes of Palm Beach," and to the White House . . . Strode's Scrapple is a delicacy that is sorely missed!

BEULAH'S LEMON CAPERS

1 large lemon
1 Bermuda onion
Anchovies
Capers
$^1/_4$ to $^1/_2$ cup extra-virgin olive oil

Slice the lemon and onion into paper thin slices and cut into quarters. Place the slices in a large jar. Cut the desired amount of anchovies into pieces and add to the jar. Drain the desired amount of capers and add to the jar. Add enough of the olive oil to cover. Marinate in the refrigerator for 8 to 12 hours. The mixture will keep in the refrigerator for several days. Serve on sturdy crackers or bread slices. Be sure that some of each ingredient is on each cracker. Yield: 15 servings.

Nutritional information for this recipe is not available.

 3/27/1897—The cows have gone forth into the meadows, but not to feed upon the pretty daisies and sweet scented clover, but upon the rank, coarse tussies of garlic which everywhere abound. How do we know it? Taste your butter and if you pronounce it even fair, you have regards for your butter man's feelings which prevent you from telling all you think. He doesn't deserve your sympathy . . . How to prevent it? Keep your cows in the barn until April or lower your price.

—*Morning Republican*

*RADISH SPREAD

1 cup radishes
8 ounces cream cheese, softened
1 garlic clove
6 tablespoons lemon juice
3/4 teaspoon salt
1/2 teaspoon dried dillweed
Pepper to taste

Scrub the radishes and dry completely. Combine the radishes, cream cheese, garlic, lemon juice, salt, dillweed and pepper in a food processor and process until the mixture is creamy. Place in a small bowl. Garnish with parsley and radish slices. Chill, covered, until serving time.
Yield: 8 servings.

Approx Per Serving: Cal 106; Prot 2 g; Carbo 3 g; T Fat 10 g; 82% Calories from Fat; Chol 31 mg; Fiber <1 g; Sod 308 mg

6/10/1899—The sweltering weather of the past week had a tendency to lessen the cravings of the human appetite for food, particularly that of the stronger varieties. People dragged themselves to the table with a sort of don't care manner, and withdrew with one-half the quantity consumed which they put away when the blizzard raged and they plunged through ten feet snow drifts last winter. It is hard for the housewife to know just what to purchase and prepare to please the rather fastidious appetites of those for whom she feels it is a duty to cater.

—Morning Republican

*ASPARAGUS SPEARS

2 pounds thin fresh asparagus spears
1 (16-ounce) package phyllo dough
1/2 cup melted butter
1 pound thinly sliced prosciutto
1/2 cup (about) grated Parmesan cheese

Snap any tough ends from the asparagus. Blanch the asparagus in boiling water in a saucepan until the spears turn a rich green color and are tender-crisp. Rinse under cold running water to stop the cooking process. Thaw the phyllo dough. Follow the directions on the package for handling and to prevent drying. Place 2 sheets of phyllo together, brushing each sheet lightly with the butter. Cut the phyllo into squares, approximately 6×6 inches in size. Cut the prosciutto slices in half. Wrap each asparagus spear in a half slice of prosciutto, place on a square of phyllo, sprinkle with Parmesan cheese and roll up to enclose the filling, leaving the ends of the asparagus slightly exposed. Arrange the rolls on a baking sheet and brush with melted butter. Bake at 400 degrees for 10 to 12 minutes or until golden brown. Yield: 30 servings.

Approx Per Serving: Cal 114; Prot 5 g; Carbo 10 g; T Fat 6 g; 48% Calories from Fat; Chol 18 mg; Fiber 1 g; Sod 335 mg

 In 1703 a jury was appointed to locate and build a public road from the Schuylkill River to Goshen meeting, crossing all of Chester County from east to west.

Prior to 1774 Humphrey Marshall (Marshall Square) built the first greenhouse in Chester County.

*STUFFED MUSHROOMS

24 button mushrooms
1/4 cup finely chopped green, red or yellow bell pepper
1/2 cup finely chopped onion   1/4 teaspoon seasoned salt
1 cup bread crumbs
1/2 cup finely chopped cooked sausage or pepperoni
1/4 cup grated Parmesan cheese   1/2 cup finely shredded Cheddar cheese

Remove the stems from the mushrooms and chop finely. Combine with the bell pepper, onion, salt, bread crumbs, sausage and Parmesan cheese in a bowl and toss until well mixed. Press the mixture into the mushroom caps and arrange in a lightly greased baking dish. Top with the Cheddar cheese. Bake at 300 degrees for 20 minutes or until the cheese is melted. Yield: 24 servings.

Approx Per Serving: Cal 40; Prot 2 g; Carbo 4 g; T Fat 2 g; 34% Calories from Fat;
Chol 4 mg; Fiber <1 g; Sod 90 mg

*ITALIAN-STYLE ROASTED PEPPERS

2 cups chopped Roasted Red Peppers
1/4 cup extra-virgin olive oil   2 garlic cloves, minced
1 tablespoon chopped parsley   Salt and pepper to taste

Combine the Roasted Red Peppers with the remaining ingredients in a bowl. Refrigerate until serving time. Serve with Italian bread and sharp provolone cheese. Yield: 10 servings.

Approx Per Serving: Cal 79; Prot 1 g; Carbo 5 g; T Fat 6 g; 68% Calories from Fat;
Chol 0 mg; Fiber 1 g; Sod 339 mg

ROASTED RED PEPPERS

Rinse whole peppers and make a small slit in the side of each. Roast or grill over medium to high heat until the skin is charred, turning to roast on all sides. Place in a covered pan to steam. Discard the stems, skin and membranes with seeds; do not rinse or flavor will be lost. Package in freezer bags for storage.

BLEU CHEESE CRISPS

8 ounces bleu cheese, crumbled
1/2 cup butter or margarine, softened
1 1/3 cups flour
1/3 cup poppy seeds
1/4 teaspoon red pepper

Combine the bleu cheese and butter in a mixing bowl and beat until fluffy. Add the flour, poppy seeds and red pepper and mix until blended. Divide the mixture into 2 portions and shape each into a 9-inch log. Wrap each log tightly and refrigerate for 2 hours to overnight. Cut the logs into 1/4-inch slices and arrange on a baking sheet. Bake at 350 degrees for 13 to 15 minutes or until golden brown. Yield: 72 crisps.

Approx Per Crisp: Cal 34; Prot 1 g; Carbo 2 g; T Fat 3 g; 65% Calories from Fat;
Chol 6 mg; Fiber <1 g; Sod 57 mg

*CHEESE ALMOND FINGERS

2 cups shredded Cheddar cheese
6 slices crisp-cooked bacon, crumbled
4 ounces slivered almonds
1 onion, finely chopped
1 cup mayonnaise
Pepper to taste
16 thin slices white bread

Combine the cheese, bacon, almonds, onion, mayonnaise and pepper in a bowl and mix well. Cut the crusts from the bread and cut each slice into thirds lengthwise. Spread the bread with the cheese mixture and arrange on baking sheets. Freeze until firm and store in plastic bags in the freezer. Arrange the frozen cheese fingers on a baking sheet. Bake at 400 degrees for 10 minutes or until golden brown. Yield: 48 servings.

Approx Per Serving: Cal 100; Prot 3 g; Carbo 5 g; T Fat 7 g; 68% Calories from Fat;
Chol 9 mg; Fiber <1 g; Sod 112 mg

*CHILES RELLENOS

2 (7-ounce) cans whole green chiles
2 cups shredded Cheddar cheese
2¹/2 cups shredded Monterey Jack cheese
4 eggs, beaten   ¹/3 cup flour   1³/4 cups milk
1 teaspoon salt   ¹/4 teaspoon ground cumin
2 or 3 drops of Tabasco sauce

Arrange the chiles in a greased 8×12-inch baking dish. Sprinkle the cheeses over the chiles. Combine the eggs, flour, milk, salt, cumin and Tabasco sauce in a mixing bowl and beat until well blended. Pour the mixture over the cheeses. Bake at 350 degrees for 45 minutes or until set and golden brown. Cool slightly and cut into squares to serve as appetizers. Yield: 60 servings.

Approx Per Serving: Cal 46; Prot 3 g; Carbo 1 g; T Fat 3 g; 64% Calories from Fat; Chol 23 mg; Fiber <1 g; Sod 173 mg

---

*BROILED CRAB MELTAWAYS

1 (6-count) package English muffins
1 (6-ounce) can crab meat
¹/2 cup margarine, softened
1 (5-ounce) jar Old English sharp Cheddar cheese spread
2 tablespoons mayonnaise
¹/2 teaspoon seasoned salt
¹/2 teaspoon garlic salt

Split the English muffins and cut each half into quarters. Arrange the muffin pieces on baking sheets. Drain the crab meat and flake into a mixing bowl. Add the margarine, cheese spread, mayonnaise, seasoned salt and garlic salt and beat at medium speed until well mixed. Spread on the English muffin pieces. Freeze for at least 30 minutes even if planning to use immediately. Broil until puffed and golden brown. Serve hot. Yield: 48 servings.

Approx Per Serving: Cal 51; Prot 2 g; Carbo 3 g; T Fat 3 g; 60% Calories from Fat; Chol 6 mg; Fiber <1 g; Sod 143 mg

*SHRIMP PITA WEDGES

8 ounces shrimp, cooked, peeled
2 tablespoons fresh lemon juice
8 ounces cream cheese, softened
1 cup shredded sharp Cheddar cheese
4 green onions, chopped
2 garlic cloves, minced
2 tablespoons chopped parsley
1 teaspoon ground cumin
1 teaspoon chili powder
6 pita bread rounds

Place the shrimp in a bowl and sprinkle with the lemon juice. Chill, covered, for 30 minutes. Combine the shrimp, cream cheese, Cheddar cheese, green onions, garlic, parsley, cumin and chili powder in a food processor. Process for about 1 minute or until smooth.

Split each of the pita bread rounds into 2 halves and cut each into 6 wedges. Spread the wedges with the shrimp mixture and arrange on baking sheets.

Bake at 350 degrees for 10 minutes or until bubbly. Garnish with additional parsley.
Yield: 72 servings.

Approx Per Serving: Cal 34; Prot 2 g; Carbo 3 g; T Fat 2 g; 46% Calories from Fat;
Chol 9 mg; Fiber <1 g; Sod 51 mg

2/26/1898—The flower stand of late has grown to be an attractive feature of the markets. That maiden whose friend wears those pretty scented violets each Saturday evening may be found among the Friday evening market goers.

—*Morning Republican*

*VEAL MEDALLIONS WITH APRICOT HORSERADISH SAUCE

1 1/2 pounds veal cutlets
Salt and pepper to taste
3 eggs
2 tablespoons milk
1/2 teaspoon salt
1/4 teaspoon pepper
2 cups fine bread crumbs
3 cups vegetable oil for frying
Apricot Horseradish Sauce

Cut the veal cutlets into bite-size pieces and sprinkle with salt and pepper to taste. Beat the eggs with milk, 1/2 teaspoon salt and 1/4 teaspoon pepper in a bowl. Dip each veal piece into the egg mixture and roll in the bread crumbs to coat. Fry in hot oil in a skillet until golden brown. Drain on paper towels. Serve with the Apricot Horseradish Sauce for dipping. Yield: 50 servings.

APRICOT HORSERADISH SAUCE

1 (12-ounce) jar apricot preserves
1 (8-ounce) jar horseradish sauce

Combine the apricot preserves and horseradish in a blender and process until well mixed.

Approx Per Serving: Cal 79; Prot 4 g; Carbo 8 g; T Fat 3 g; 38% Calories from Fat;
Chol 27 mg; Fiber <1 g; Sod 90 mg
Nutritional information does not include the oil for frying.

ROASTED EGGPLANT CHEESECAKE

1 medium eggplant   5 garlic cloves   1 cup canned tomatoes
1 teaspoon dried thyme $1/4$ teaspoon salt $1/4$ teaspoon pepper
32 ounces cream cheese, softened   3 eggs   Pine Nut Crust   Cream Sauce

Pierce the eggplant all over with a fork and rub with a small amount of vegetable oil. Place the eggplant and unpeeled garlic cloves on a baking sheet. Bake at 350 degrees for 1 hour or until very soft. Cut the eggplant into halves and scoop out the pulp. Drain the pulp and place in a food processor. Add about $1/4$ of the eggplant skin. Squeeze the garlic pulp into the eggplant mixture. Add the tomatoes, thyme, salt and pepper and process until smooth. Beat the cream cheese in a mixing bowl until very smooth. Add the eggs 1 at a time, beating until smooth after each addition. Fold in the eggplant mixture and beat until well blended. Pour into the Pine Nut Crust. Bake at 350 degrees for 40 minutes. Rotate the pan $1/2$ turn. Bake for 35 minutes longer or until a wooden pick inserted in the center comes out clean. Cool slightly. Loosen the cheesecake from the side of the pan. Remove the side of the pan. Cut into wedges and place on serving plates. Serve warm with the Cream Sauce. Yield: 12 servings.

PINE NUT CRUST

$1/2$ cup pine nuts, toasted   1 cup bread crumbs
2 tablespoons butter, softened   1 garlic clove, roasted

Process the pine nuts and bread crumbs in a food processor until of the consistency of coarse crumbs. Add the butter and garlic and mix until crumbly. Press evenly over the bottom of a 10-inch springform pan. You may substitute your favorite nut for the pine nuts.

CREAM SAUCE

1 cup heavy cream $1/4$ cup grated Parmesan cheese
Salt and pepper to taste   Puréed garlic to taste (optional)

Pour the cream into a shallow pan. Bring to a simmer. Simmer until the volume of the cream is reduced by half. Whisk in the Parmesan cheese. Add salt, pepper and puréed garlic.

Approx Per Serving: Cal 463; Prot 12 g; Carbo 14 g; T Fat 41 g; 78% Calories from Fat; Chol 170 mg; Fiber 2 g; Sod 463 mg

*CURRIED WALNUTS

1 pound walnut halves   1/2 cup sugar
2 1/2 tablespoons vegetable oil   1/2 teaspoon salt
1/2 teaspoon pepper   1/4 teaspoon cayenne pepper
1 1/4 teaspoons ground cumin   1/4 teaspoon coriander
1/2 teaspoon ginger   1/4 teaspoon cloves
1/2 teaspoon chili powder

Blanch the walnuts in boiling water for 1 minute and drain well. Combine the hot walnuts with sugar and oil in a large bowl and toss until well mixed. Let stand for 10 minutes. Spread the walnuts in a single layer in a large shallow baking pan. Bake at 325 degrees for 30 minutes or until brown and crispy, turning every 5 to 10 minutes. Place the walnuts in a large bowl. Sprinkle with the salt, pepper, cayenne pepper, cumin, coriander, ginger, cloves and chili powder and toss until well mixed. Spread in a single layer on paper towels to cool. Yield: 16 servings.

Approx Per Serving: Cal 225; Prot 4 g; Carbo 11 g; T Fat 20 g; 74% Calories from Fat;
Chol 0 mg; Fiber 1 g; Sod 76 mg

*BISHOP'S DOWNFALL

12 oranges
Whole cloves
8 gallons cider   Cinnamon sticks
1 gallon dark rum
Nutmeg

Stud the oranges generously with the cloves. Place the oranges on a baking sheet. Roast the oranges at 375 degrees for 1 hour. Heat the cider with the cinnamon sticks in a large kettle. Place the hot oranges in a punchbowl. Add the rum and the hot cider. Remove the cinnamon sticks. Sprinkle with nutmeg. Yield: 200 servings.

Approx Per Serving: Cal 116; Prot <1 g; Carbo 19 g; T Fat <1 g; 1% Calories from Fat;
Chol 0 mg; Fiber <1 g; Sod 5 mg
Nutritional information is for the cider and rum only.

SAM TWINING'S BLUEBERRY TEA

1 ounce amaretto
5 ounces prepared Twinings Ceylon Breakfast Tea
1 ounce Grand Marnier

Warm 2 wine glasses. Divide the Amaretto between the glasses. Divide the tea between the glasses and add half the Grand Marnier to each glass. Serve immediately. Yield: 2 servings.

Approx Per Serving: Cal 83; Prot <1 g; Carbo 6 g; T Fat <1 g; 0% Calories from Fat;
Chol 0 mg; Fiber 0 g; Sod 1 mg

*SAM TWINING'S ICED TEA

Twinings Ceylon Breakfast or
Black Current Tea
Sugar   Ice
Bruised mint, lemon slices or cucumber borage

Brew the tea according to the package directions, using 1 additional teabag. Combine the desired amount of sugar and ice in a pitcher. Add the hot tea, stir until the sugar dissolves and top up the pitcher with cold water. Refrigerate for 4 hours. Serve in tall glasses with ice and mint, lemon, or borage. Yield: variable.

Nutritional information for this recipe is not available.

*PEMBROKE PUNCH

2 (16-ounce) cans frozen lemonade concentrate
6 lemonade cans light dry sherry
Ice Ring

Thaw the lemonade concentrate in a large container and reconstitute according to the package directions substituting sherry for the water. Chill until serving time. Pour the lemonade into a punchbowl. Invert the mold to remove the ice ring. Place the Ice Ring carefully in the lemonade. This recipe is courtesy of the Pembroke College Alumni Association. Yield: 25 servings.

Approx Per Serving: Cal 160; Prot <1 g; Carbo 19 g; T Fat <1 g; 0% Calories from Fat; Chol 0 mg; Fiber <1 g; Sod 15 mg

ICE RING

Use cherries and holly for Christmas or strawberries in spring and summer. Spray a ring mold with nonstick cooking spray. Arrange the fruit in the mold and add a small amount of water carefully to avoid dislodging the fruit. Freeze until firm.

Add additional fruit if desired and a small amount of water. Freeze until firm. Continue adding water gradually and freezing with each addition. Adding water gradually keeps the fruit on the bottom of the ring so that when the ice ring is inverted in the punchbowl the fruit or other decorations are on the top.

Priscilla Moore Robinson, who ran the Blue Bell Tavern near Paoli, lived to the age of 100. She was called "Old Prissy" by neighboring children, and her ghost is thought to inhabit the inn which is now a private residence.

HUMMER

4 scoops vanilla or coffee ice cream
1 ounce light rum
1 ounce Kahlúa
1 ounce brandy
1 ounce crème de cacao

Combine the ice cream, rum, Kahlúa, brandy and crème de cacao in a blender and process until smooth. Pour into brandy snifters. Yield: 2 servings.

Approx Per Serving: Cal 434; Prot 5 g; Carbo 43 g; T Fat 15 g; 30% Calories from Fat;
Chol 58 mg; Fiber 0 g; Sod 108 mg

MOCHA PUNCH

1^1/2 quarts water
^{1}/2 cup instant chocolate drink mix
^{1}/2 cup sugar
^{1}/4 cup instant coffee granules
^{1}/2 gallon vanilla ice cream
^{1}/2 gallon chocolate ice cream
1 cup whipped cream

Bring the water to a boil in a large saucepan. Remove from the heat and add the drink mix, sugar and coffee granules and stir until completely dissolved. Let stand until cool. Refrigerate in a covered container for 4 hours to overnight. Pour the mixture into a punchbowl about 30 minutes before serving time. Add the ice cream by scoopfuls and stir gently until the ice cream is partially melted. Top with dollops of whipped cream and garnish with chocolate curls. Yield: 10 servings.

Approx Per Serving: Cal 542; Prot 8 g; Carbo 70 g; T Fat 28 g; 44% Calories from Fat;
Chol 98 mg; Fiber 2 g; Sod 198 mg

*WALDEMUSTER (MAY WINE)

1 cup fresh woodruff
2 bottles of Rhine or Moselle wine
$^1/_2$ cup peach brandy
1 cup superfine sugar   1 or 2 oranges
1 quart Champagne or soda
1 pint fresh strawberries
Ice Ring (page 31)

Rinse the woodruff and pat dry. Place the woodruff, wine, brandy and sugar in a large container. Let stand, covered, for several hours to overnight. Strain the mixture into a punchbowl. Peel the oranges and separate into sections. Add the oranges and Champagne and stir gently. Place the Ice Ring in the punchbowl. Place the strawberries in individual cups before adding the punch.
Yield: 30 servings.

Approx Per Serving: Cal 97; Prot <1 g; Carbo 9 g; T Fat <1 g; 0% Calories from Fat;
Chol 0 mg; Fiber <1 g; Sod 4 mg

WASSAIL

8 ounces fresh cranberries
2 lemons, sliced
1 orange, sliced   2 quarts water
$^1/_2$ to $^3/_4$ cup sugar
1 (46-ounce) can grapefruit juice
16 whole cloves   3 cinnamon sticks

Combine the cranberries, lemons and orange in a large saucepan. Add the water and cook until the cranberries pop. Add sugar to taste and mix until the sugar dissolves. Add the grapefruit juice, cloves and cinnamon sticks and heat to serving temperature. Strain into punch cups.
Yield: 12 servings.

Approx Per Serving: Cal 108; Prot 1 g; Carbo 29 g; T Fat <1 g; 2% Calories from Fat;
Chol 0 mg; Fiber 2 g; Sod 2 mg

"A DUZON OF DELF PLEATS"

In early 1738 an interesting occurrence took place in southern Chester County in the New Garden and London Grove areas. A group of approximately twelve Quaker families got together and decided to place a group order for Delftware plates from a merchant in Philadelphia. The plates illustrated here, all in the collection of CCHS, are surviving representatives of five of the sets ordered.

The merchant in Philadelphia—probably a Quaker, but we do not know his identity—would have been an agent for one of the finest potteries in England. Perhaps he had samples from which the families could choose when they placed their order. The surviving plates are of four different designs: the William Gregg family and William and Elizabeth Lewis ordered plates of the same design, while Joseph and Sara Dixon, the John Allen family, and the William Beverley family chose other designs. All the plates are dated 1738 and marked with the initials of either the husband or the husband and wife. The fact that they are all dated the same and that the manufacturing technique is identical adds to the evidence that it was a group order.

Although most of the families were of Irish descent, it appears they chose an English pottery from which to commission their plates; the reddish brown edges of the plates indicate a Liverpool connection. All imported Delftware was expensive, however, and only the wealthiest families in Chester County could have afforded such a luxury. The survival of these five plates is indicative of the importance accorded them: family records and inventories indicate that the sets of plates were divided among the various children of the couples who had ordered them.

The plates give witness to a remarkable level of sophistication and social awareness in southern Chester County in the early 18th century. The families ordering these handsome Delft plates lived in a decidedly rural area, but they were aware of, and aspired to, the same level of refinement as their Quaker counterparts in Philadelphia.

At John Allen's death in 1771, his inventory included "a Duzon of Delf pleats."

Point to Point Tailgate Picnic

Hoagie Dip with Crackers
(PAGE 12)

Cheese Spread with Pretzel Logs
(PAGE 18)

Chiles Rellenos
(PAGE 25)

Mushroom Soup and French Bread
(PAGE 41)

Easter Asparagus
(PAGE 46)

Marinated Vegetable Salad
(PAGE 50)

Granny's Red Cabbage Salad
(PAGE 47)

Chocolate Pizza
(PAGE 169)

Vinegar Cookies
(PAGE 164)

Waldemuster (May Wine) or Twinings Lemon Tea Iced
(PAGE 33)

*APPLE SQUASH BISQUE

Pace One Restaurant

5 apples
1 (2-pound) butternut squash
11 cups chicken stock
1 1/2 large onions, chopped
1 teaspoon dried rosemary
1 cup margarine
1 cup flour
1/3 cup sugar
3/4 cup apple cider
4 cups half-and-half

Peel and core the apples and set aside. Peel and seed enough of the squash to yield 1 1/2 pounds. Chop the apples and squash into same size pieces. Combine the apples, squash and chicken stock in a large stock pot. Add the onions and rosemary. Bring to a boil and reduce the heat. Simmer, covered, for 20 minutes. Blend the margarine and flour in a saucepan. Cook over medium heat until the mixture bubbles, stirring constantly. Whisk the roux into the squash mixture until well mixed. Add the sugar and cider and whisk until well mixed. Cook until thickened, whisking constantly. Remove from the heat and blend in the half-and-half. Serve immediately.
Yield: 20 servings.

Approx Per Serving: Cal 230; Prot 3 g; Carbo 22 g; T Fat 15 g; 58% Calories from Fat;
Chol 18 mg; Fiber 2 g; Sod 505 mg

 Chester County Inventor . . . Moses Coates, (1745–1816) of Coatesville, in Chester Valley patented the APPLE PARING MACHINE (1803), and with some slight modification is still in use today. Moses also invented a self setting SAW MILL and claimed the invention of a HORSE RAKE.

SENATE BEAN SOUP

1 cup dried navy beans
1 1/2 quarts water
1 meaty ham hock
1/4 cup instant mashed potato flakes
1 1/2 cups finely chopped onions
3 ribs celery with leaves, finely chopped
1 garlic clove, pressed
2 tablespoons chopped parsley
Salt and pepper to taste

Sort and rinse the beans. Place the beans in a large saucepan and add the water. Let the beans soak for 8 to 12 hours. Add the ham hock and bring the mixture to a boil. Reduce the heat and simmer, covered, for about 1 hour or until the beans begin to soften, adding small amounts of hot water as necessary. Stir in the potato flakes. Add the onions, celery, garlic and parsley. Simmer for 1 hour or until the beans are very tender, adding small amounts of hot water as necessary; soup should be thick. Add salt and pepper. Serve with hot bread and a crisp salad. Yield: 4 servings.

Approx Per Serving: Cal 239; Prot 17 g; Carbo 36 g; T Fat 3 g; 12% Calories from Fat; Chol 14 mg; Fiber 19 g; Sod 80 mg

Charles Lindbergh was a surprise overnight guest in Chester County in March, 1928, less than a year after his historic non-stop flight across the Atlantic. Forced by fog to land in a field, Lindbergh spent the night at the farm of Charles Elkinton and was treated to a hero's send-off the next morning by cheering county residents.

BROCCOLI SOUP

2 large stalks broccoli
1 carrot
^{1}/2 medium onion, chopped
2 tablespoons butter
1^1/2 tablespoons flour
Salt and pepper to taste
2 cups half-and-half
^{1}/2 (14-ounce) can chicken broth
^{1}/2 cup dry sherry
Garlic salt to taste

Discard woody portions of broccoli. Chop the broccoli and carrot. Cook the broccoli and carrot in a small amount of water in a saucepan until tender, drain and set aside. Sauté the onion in butter in a large saucepan until tender. Add the flour and mix well. Season with salt and pepper. Add the half-and-half and cook until thickened, stirring constantly. Add the broth, sherry, garlic salt and cooked broccoli and carrot mixture. Heat the soup to serving temperature, stirring gently.
Yield: 8 servings.

Approx Per Serving: Cal 137; Prot 4 g; Carbo 6 g; T Fat 10 g; 65% Calories from Fat;
Chol 30 mg; Fiber 1 g; Sod 216 mg

 Harry A. Longabaugh, who became known as the Sundance Kid, was born in 1867 near Phoenixville in Chester County. He learned to ride horses at the Wilmer Ralston farm in west Vincent Township where he went to work at the age of 13.

CHEESY CHICKEN CHOWDER

2 cups chopped peeled potatoes
1 cup chopped carrots
1 cup chopped celery
$1/2$ cup chopped onion
3 cups chicken broth
$1^1/2$ teaspoons salt
$1/4$ teaspoon pepper
$1/4$ cup butter
$1/3$ cup flour
2 cups milk
2 cups shredded Cheddar or Velveeta cheese
2 cups chopped cooked chicken or turkey

Combine the potatoes, carrots, celery and onion in a large saucepan. Add the broth, salt and pepper. Bring to a simmer and simmer, covered, until the vegetables are tender.

Melt the butter in a medium saucepan over low heat. Blend in the flour. Cook for several minutes, stirring constantly. Stir in the milk gradually and cook until thickened, stirring constantly.

Add the cheese and cook until the cheese melts, stirring constantly. Stir the cheese mixture into the vegetable mixture. Add the chicken and mix gently. Heat to serving temperature over low heat, stirring constantly. Yield: 8 servings.

Approx Per Serving: Cal 345; Prot 23 g; Carbo 17 g; T Fat 20 g; 53% Calories from Fat; Chol 85 mg; Fiber 2 g; Sod 1042 mg

*MUSHROOM SOUP

2 leeks
1/4 cup unsalted butter
1 teaspoon minced garlic
2 pounds white mushrooms, sliced
1/2 teaspoon salt
1 potato, peeled, chopped
2 ribs celery, chopped
4 cups chicken stock
1 recipe Boursin Cheese (page 17) or 1 (8-ounce) package boursin cheese
3 tablespoons Calvados
1 1/2 teaspoons fresh lemon juice
1 tablespoons chopped fresh chervil leaves
1 teaspoon salt
1/2 teaspoon freshly ground pepper

Trim the leeks, split lengthwise and rinse well. Drain and slice thinly. Melt the butter in a large saucepan over medium heat. Add the leeks and cook for 3 minutes or until tender, stirring frequently. Add the garlic and cook for 2 minutes. Add the mushrooms and 1/2 teaspoon salt. Cook for 5 minutes or until the mushrooms begin to soften, stirring frequently. Add the potato, celery and chicken stock. Bring to a boil and reduce the heat to low. Simmer, covered, for 30 minutes or until the potatoes are tender.

Purée the mushroom mixture in batches in a food processor or blender. Return the soup to the saucepan. Crumble the cheese and add to the saucepan. Whisk until well blended. Add the Calvados, lemon juice, chervil, 1 teaspoon salt and pepper and whisk until well blended. Heat to serving temperature, stirring frequently. Yield: 10 servings.

Approx Per Serving: Cal 220; Prot 6 g; Carbo 10 g; T Fat 17 g; 68% Calories from Fat;
Chol 50 mg; Fiber 2 g; Sod 781 mg

*OYSTER STEW

1 pint shucked oysters with liquor
1 quart milk
1 tablespoon minced onion
1 teaspoon white wine Worcestershire sauce
1 1/2 cups sliced mushrooms
1 tablespoon butter
Salt and pepper to taste

Preparation of this recipe requires 3 operations in 3 separate pans. Contents of all of the pans should be ready to combine at the same time. Place the oysters with liquor in a small saucepan over low to medium heat until the edges of the oysters begin to curl. Heat the milk, onion and Worcestershire sauce in a large saucepan over medium heat just until simmering. Sauté the mushrooms in the butter in a skillet until the mushrooms are tender. Add the oysters and sautéed mushrooms to the milk mixture and mix well. Serve in soup bowls with oyster crackers.
Yield: 6 servings.

Approx Per Serving: Cal 181; Prot 12 g; Carbo 12 g; T Fat 9 g; 47% Calories from Fat;
Chol 73 mg; Fiber <1 g; Sod 202 mg

11/14/1896—The oyster man wears a worried look, for oysters in the height of their season are said to be scarce. It's a mean oyster which sells for 60 cents per hundred.
—*Morning Republican*

FORTIFYING HOT OR COLD ZUCCHINI SOUP

6 small or 3 medium zucchini
2 large onions
2 tablespoons olive oil
2 tablespoons butter
1 (48-ounce) can chicken broth
1 tablespoon chopped fresh parsley
1 tablespoon chopped fresh dill
1 tablespoon chopped fresh basil
Salt and pepper to taste

Slice the zucchini and onions. Heat the olive oil and butter in a large soup pot over low heat until the butter melts. Add the zucchini and onions. Cook, covered, until the vegetables are very tender but not brown. Add the broth and parsley, dill and basil. Simmer for 10 minutes. Process the zucchini mixture in a blender or food processor until the vegetables are finely chopped but do not purée. Return the soup to the soup pot if the soup is to served hot. Add salt and pepper and heat to serving temperature. Ladle into soup bowls and garnish with snipped dill, chives or other fresh herbs. If the soup is to be served cold, chill in the refrigerator until serving time, adjust the seasonings, pour into soup bowls and garnish with herbs. Yield: 8 servings.

Approx Per Serving: Cal 133; Prot 9 g; Carbo 7 g; T Fat 8 g; 54% Calories from Fat;
Chol 9 mg; Fiber 2 g; Sod 1098 mg

William Penn originally had chosen the town of Chester (called Upland in the late 17th century) which was then part of Chester County, as the site for his "Greene Country Town." However, the Swedes had settled the area over thirty years earlier, and the price of real estate was too dear for Penn's budget. He then chose a site more inland on the Delaware River and established Philadelphia as his capital of Pennsylvania.

*APPLE-SPINACH SALAD

2 (6-ounce) packages fresh baby spinach
2 Granny Smith apples
$1/2$ cup salted cashews
$1/4$ cup golden raisins
Sweet Oil and Vinegar Dressing

Rinse the spinach well and pat dry. Core and chop the apples. Combine the spinach, apples, cashews and raisins in a salad bowl. Pour the Sweet Oil and Vinegar Dressing over the salad and toss gently to mix. Serve immediately. Yield: 4 servings.

SWEET OIL AND VINEGAR DRESSING

$1/4$ cup sugar
$1/4$ teaspoon celery salt
$1/4$ teaspoon garlic salt
3 tablespoons apple cider vinegar
$1/4$ cup vegetable oil

Combine the sugar, celery and garlic salts in a small bowl. Add the vinegar and mix well. Add the oil gradually, whisking constantly until well blended. May refrigerate the dressing in a covered container for 8 to 12 hours. Mix well before adding to the salad.

Approx Per Serving: Cal 341; Prot 6 g; Carbo 36 g; T Fat 22 g; 54% Calories from Fat;
Chol 0 mg; Fiber 5 g; Sod 377 mg
Nutritional information includes the entire amount of the Sweet Oil and Vinegar Dressing.

*MINTED MELON AND GRAPEFRUIT

1 (2¹/₄-pound) cantaloupe
2 pink grapefruit
1 white grapefruit
1 teaspoon Dijon mustard
1¹/₂ teaspoons raspberry or sherry vinegar
1 teaspoon honey
1¹/₂ tablespoons chopped fresh mint

Discard the cantaloupe seeds and scoop the pulp into balls with a melon baller. Peel and section the grapefruit over a large bowl to retain all juices. Remove and discard the membranes. Add the mustard, vinegar, honey and mint to the grapefruit juice and mix well. Add the melon balls and grapefruit sections to the bowl and mix gently. Chill for 30 minutes. Scoop the fruit into glass dishes and garnish with fresh mint sprigs. Yield: 4 servings.

Approx Per Serving: Cal 112; Prot 2 g; Carbo 27 g; T Fat 1 g; 5% Calories from Fat;
Chol 0 mg; Fiber 3 g; Sod 43 mg
Nutritional information includes the entire amount of the dressing.

 5/27/1922—Referring to the good old times—"Sociability in those good old times was of the kind that washed well, 'cause it was without veneer. A neighbor was a helper always, and family sympathy for the whole neighboring community was without stint. It was a good thing for one and all to meet at church, and at the annual picnic, where wholesome wives and daughters vied with each other in supplying cakes. Devil's food and angel food cake had not yet been discovered, but the sponge cake and the cookie were just as attractive, mainly because they were of a better texture and flavor. Ah! Those good old times! Those days when "sassiety" had not yet trampled upon the toes of good citizenship.

*EASTER ASPARAGUS

3 pounds fresh asparagus spears
2 tablespoons fresh lemon juice
2 tablespoons red wine vinegar
1 tablespoon minced onion
1 small garlic clove, minced
1/2 teaspoon salt
1/4 teaspoon Dijon mustard
1 cup olive oil

Snap the tough ends from the asparagus. Steam the asparagus just until tender-crisp, rinse with cold water to stop the cooking process and drain well. Chill the asparagus until serving time. Place the asparagus on a serving platter. Combine the lemon juice, vinegar, onion, garlic, salt and mustard in a small bowl or jar and mix well. Whisk the olive oil into the bowl gradually or add the olive oil to the jar, cover and shake vigorously. Drizzle the dressing over the asparagus and serve immediately. Yield: 10 servings.

Approx Per Serving: Cal 226; Prot 3 g; Carbo 7 g; T Fat 22 g; 83% Calories from Fat;
Chol 0 mg; Fiber 3 g; Sod 122 mg
Nutritional information includes the entire amount of the dressing.

6/5/1897—Old, tough, asparagus is not the dish it was two weeks ago. Some folks say that the new string beans are tough too. To the former, it's good-bye for another year, but to the latter, it's wait for the Chester County produce.

—*Morning Republican*

*GRANNY'S RED CABBAGE SALAD

4 cups shredded red cabbage
4 cups watercress
2 Granny Smith apples
$1/2$ cup Double Apple Vinaigrette

Combine the cabbage and watercress in a salad bowl. Core the apples and cut into 1-inch pieces. Add to the cabbage and watercress. Add the Double Apple Vinaigrette, toss lightly and serve immediately. Yield: 6 servings

Approx Per Serving: Cal 77; Prot 1 g; Carbo 10 g; T Fat 4 g; 45% Calories from Fat; Chol 0 mg; Fiber 2 g; Sod 101 mg

DOUBLE APPLE VINAIGRETTE

$3/4$ cup unsweetened applesauce
$1/4$ cup apple cider vinegar
1 tablespoon Dijon mustard
2 large scallions, quartered
$1/2$ teaspoon salt
$1/3$ cup olive oil

Combine the applesauce, vinegar, mustard, scallions and salt in a blender or food processor. Process until smooth. Add the olive oil in a fine stream, processing constantly. Store the unused vinaigrette in a covered container in the refrigerator for up to 1 week. Yield: 3 ($1/2$-cup) portions.

Approx Per Portion: Cal 252; Prot 1 g; Carbo 8 g; T Fat 24 g; 86% Calories from Fat; Chol 0 mg; Fiber 1 g; Sod 518 mg

*COOL CARROT AND PINEAPPLE SALAD

2 pounds carrots
Salt to taste
1 green bell pepper
1 medium onion, chopped
1 (16-ounce) can pineapple chunks, drained
1 (10-ounce) can low-sodium tomato soup
1/4 cup canola oil
3/4 cup sugar
2 teaspoons Dijon mustard
3/4 cup cider vinegar

Slice the carrots crosswise as for copper pennies. Cook the carrots in a small amount of salted water in a covered saucepan just until tender-crisp or place the carrots in a covered 3-quart microwave-safe casserole with a small amount of water and microwave on High for 4 minutes. Cut the green pepper into desired size pieces. Drain the carrots and combine with the green pepper, onion and pineapple chunks in a large bowl. Combine the soup, canola oil, sugar, mustard and vinegar in a saucepan and blend well. Bring the mixture to a boil, stirring until the sugar dissolves completely. Pour the hot mixture over the carrot mixture and mix gently until coated. Chill the mixture until serving time. Yield: 10 servings.

Approx Per Serving: Cal 190; Prot 2 g; Carbo 35 g; T Fat 6 g; 27% Calories from Fat;
Chol 0 mg; Fiber 4 g; Sod 64 mg

It would appear at first hand that there are already too many cook and recipe books on the market. This we believe to be far from true, for it is pretty generally accepted that "we are what we eat." We pay our doctors well to have them tell us these things and then keep on eating what we like as long as possible.

—From *Cooking with the Pennsylvania Dutch*

*CHINESE CHICKEN SALAD

1 pound cooked chicken
8 ounces fresh bean sprouts
1 medium cucumber, peeled, cut into julienne strips
2 large carrots, peeled, cut into julienne strips
Tahini Dressing

Cut the chicken into bite-size strips. Combine the chicken, bean sprouts, cucumber and carrots in a salad bowl and toss to mix. Add the desired amount of Tahini Dressing, toss lightly and serve immediately. Yield: 4 servings.

TAHINI DRESSING

3 tablespoons tahini (sesame paste)
2 scallions, chopped
2/3 cup chicken broth
3 tablespoons soy sauce
2 tablespoons rice vinegar
1 tablespoon dry sherry
2 tablespoons sesame oil
2 to 4 garlic cloves, minced
1 teaspoon sugar
1 teaspoon salt

Combine the tahini, scallions and broth in a jar, cover and shake until well mixed. Add the soy sauce, rice vinegar, sherry, sesame oil, garlic, sugar and salt and shake vigorously to mix. Store any unused dressing in the refrigerator.

Approx Per Serving: Cal 418; Prot 40 g; Carbo 15 g; T Fat 22 g; 48% Calories from Fat;
Chol 101 mg; Fiber 4 g; Sod 1820 mg
Nutritional information includes the entire amount of the Tahini Dressing.

*MARINATED VEGETABLE SALAD

1 (14-ounce) can artichoke hearts
1^1/$_2$ cups sliced carrots   3 cups chopped cauliflowerets
^{1}/$_2$ cup chopped onion
^{1}/$_2$ cup sliced celery
^{1}/$_2$ cup Italian salad dressing
^{1}/$_2$ cup mayonnaise   2 tablespoons chili sauce
1 tablespoon lemon juice
1 teaspoon dried dillweed

Drain the artichoke hearts and cut into quarters. Combine the artichokes, carrots, cauliflowerets, onion, celery and Italian salad dressing in a salad bowl and toss to mix. Chill, covered, for 2 hours or longer. Drain the vegetables. Combine the mayonnaise, chili sauce, lemon juice and dillweed in a small bowl and blend well. Pour over the vegetables and toss to mix well. Serve the vegetables on lettuce-lined salad plates. Yield: 8 servings.

Approx Per Serving: Cal 219; Prot 3 g; Carbo 12 g; T Fat 18 g; 74% Calories from Fat;
Chol 10 mg; Fiber 3 g; Sod 419 mg

*BASIL VINAIGRETTE

^{1}/$_2$ cup olive oil
3 tablespoons red or white wine vinegar
2 tablespoons fresh lemon juice
1 tablespoon Dijon country mustard
1 tablespoon chopped fresh basil
1 garlic clove, minced   Salt and pepper to taste

Combine the olive oil, wine vinegar, lemon juice, mustard, basil, garlic, salt and pepper in a jar, cover and shake vigorously to mix. Serve over a salad of Boston lettuce and radicchio with black olives and feta cheese. Yield: 14 (1-tablespoon) servings.

Approx Per Serving: Cal 72; Prot <1 g; Carbo <1 g; T Fat 8 g; 97% Calories from Fat;
Chol 0 mg; Fiber <1 g; Sod 27 mg

*SUMMER DRESSING

6 tablespoons olive oil
2 tablespoons white wine vinegar with tarragon
1 small garlic clove, minced
2 tablespoons chopped fresh parsley
2 tablespoons chopped fresh chives
1 tablespoon chopped fresh dill, or 1 teaspoon dried dill
2 teaspoons chopped fresh thyme, or $1/2$ teaspoon dried thyme
$1/2$ teaspoon salt

Combine the olive oil, vinegar, garlic, parsley, chives, dill, thyme and salt in a jar, cover and shake vigorously. Serve over a salad of mesclun and avocado. Yield: 12 (1-tablespoon) servings.

Approx Per Serving: Cal 61; Prot <1 g; Carbo <1 g; T Fat 7 g; 97% Calories from Fat;
Chol 0 mg; Fiber <1 g; Sod 97 mg

*HONEY MUSTARD DRESSING

1 cup mayonnaise
$1/2$ cup whole grain mustard
$1/2$ cup honey
2 tablespoons dry hot mustard
$3/4$ cup (about) water

Combine the mayonnaise, whole grain mustard and honey in a bowl and blend well. Add the dry mustard and mix well. Whisk in the water a little at a time to make dressing of the desired consistency. Let stand for 10 minutes to allow the flavors to develop.
Yield: 44 (1-tablespoon) servings.

Approx Per Serving: Cal 52; Prot <1 g; Carbo 3 g; T Fat 4 g; 72% Calories from Fat;
Chol 4 mg; Fiber <1 g; Sod 63 mg

"MODERATION AND PLAINNESS IN… APPAREL…"

In 1719 the Philadelphia Yearly Meeting of the Religious Society of Friends admonished its members about the lack of "moderation and plainness in gesture, speech, apparel or furniture of houses." Despite such warnings, however, Chester County Quakers, like their Philadelphia counterparts, continued throughout the 18th century and well into the 19th century to favor fine and elegant fabrics for both their personal dress and the textile furnishings in their homes. They did, however, adhere to "plainness" in both their choice of subdued colors and their formula for attire.

Plain dress for Quaker women consisted of a dress, bonnet, a small cap, a shawl, and a neckerchief. This standard dress for Quaker women persisted through the first half of the 19th century. The most striking elements that set these early female Friends apart in their dress were the solid, conservative colors in their choice of fabric. Olive green, beige, muted brown, and dove-gray silks were the favored palette among both wealthy Chester County Quakers and their urban counterparts in Philadelphia.

Most Quaker clothing that has survived from the 18th and 19th centuries is representative of the best that would have been worn by the wealthiest people. Many of the surviving dresses are silk and are documented to have been wedding dresses. In addition, many Chester County silk quilts have a history as wedding quilts, either made from scraps of wedding dresses or made before the event in anticipation of it. As can be expected, these quilts display the same muted colors but possess an elegance and fine quality of workmanship that is distinctively Quaker.

Although not all Chester Country Friends were wealthy and in possession of costly clothing and furnishings, those who were prided themselves on their wealth and social standing. Their fine but understated dress was an expression of both their worldliness and their adherence to the tenets of Quakerism.

Gala Dinner Party

Asparagus Spears
(PAGE 22)

Portobello Caviar with Crostini
(PAGE 13)

Crudités and Dill Dip

Oyster Stew with Oyster Crackers
(PAGE 42)

Green Salad with Basil Vinaigrette
(PAGE 50)

Grilled Tenderloin with Horseradish Sauce
(PAGE 55)

Swede and Carrot Mash
(PAGE 97)

Grilled Tomatoes

Browned New Potatoes

White Velvet Cheesecake Pie
(PAGE 167)

Twinings Earl Grey or Jasmine Green Tea

*GRILLED TENDERLOIN

1 (3-pound) beef tenderloin
1 1/2 cups dry red wine
3 garlic cloves, minced
2 teaspoons salt   1 teaspoon pepper
1/2 cup olive oil   Horseradish Sauce

Trim all visible fat from the tenderloin. Combine the wine, garlic, salt, pepper and olive oil in a large sealable plastic bag. Place the tenderloin in the marinade, squeeze the air from the bag and seal tightly. Marinate the tenderloin in the refrigerator for 8 to 12 hours, turning the bag occasionally. Drain the tenderloin and discard the marinade.

Grill over hot coals for about 35 minutes for medium-rare. Place the tenderloin on a serving plate and cover loosely with foil. Let rest for 5 to 10 minutes. Carve the tenderloin and serve with Horseradish Sauce. Yield: 8 servings.

HORSERADISH SAUCE

2 cups sour cream
2/3 cup prepared horseradish
White pepper and salt to taste
Lemon juice to taste

Combine the sour cream and horseradish in a bowl and mix well. Add salt and pepper and enough lemon juice to make the sauce of the desired consistency.

Approx Per Serving: Cal 551; Prot 38 g; Carbo 6 g; T Fat 38 g; 63% Calories from Fat;
Chol 131 mg; Fiber 1 g; Sod 757 mg
Nutritional information includes the entire amount of the marinade.

YANKEE POT ROAST

1 (4-pound) bottom round roast
3 tablespoons flour
2 teaspoons salt
$1/4$ teaspoon pepper
3 tablespoons vegetable oil
1 (4-ounce) jar prepared horseradish
1 (8-ounce) can jellied cranberry sauce
1 cup beef broth
1 cinnamon stick
4 whole cloves
2 onions
6 carrots

Coat the roast with a mixture of the flour, salt and pepper. Heat the oil in a Dutch oven. Add the roast and brown on all sides. Combine the horseradish, cranberry sauce and beef broth in a bowl and mix well. Break the cinnamon stick into 2 pieces. Add the cinnamon stick and whole cloves. Pour the mixture over the roast. Simmer, tightly covered, for about 2 hours or until the roast is barely tender.

Cut the onions into quarters and the carrots into 3-inch lengths and add the vegetables to the roast. Simmer, covered, for about 25 minutes or until the roast is very tender and the vegetables are tender. Remove the roast and vegetables to a serving platter. Remove the cinnamon and cloves.

May blend a small amount of water with enough flour and Kitchen Bouquet to taste to make gravy of the desired consistency and stir into the pan juices. Cook until thickened, stirring constantly. May substitute a boned, rolled arm roast or blade roast for the bottom round roast.
Yield: 12 servings.

Approx Per Serving: Cal 351; Prot 30 g; Carbo 15 g; T Fat 19 g; 48% Calories from Fat;
Chol 96 mg; Fiber 2 g; Sod 550 mg

BEEF BURGUNDY

2 pounds lean sirloin tip   2 tablespoons lemon juice
2 tablespoons olive oil   1 small onion, chopped
2 or 3 garlic cloves, minced
Salt and freshly ground pepper to taste
2 tablespoons butter
12 ounces mixed button and portobello mushrooms
12 ounces frozen small white onions, thawed
1 tablespoon tomato paste   3 tablespoons instant flour
1 cup beef bouillon   1 cup Barbera burgundy
$^1/_2$ teaspoon thyme

Cut the sirloin tip into 1-inch cubes and place in a large sealable plastic bag. Mix the lemon juice, olive oil, chopped onion, garlic, salt and pepper in a small bowl. Add to the plastic bag, squeeze the air from the bag and seal tightly. Marinate the sirloin in the refrigerator for 24 hours, turning the bag occasionally.

Melt the butter in a large heavy skillet. Add the sirloin in batches and brown on all sides over medium-high heat to avoid the formation of juices. Place the browned sirloin in a 4- to 5-quart casserole. Cut the mushrooms into quarters. Add the mushrooms and the whole onions to the skillet and cook until the vegetables are coated with the pan drippings. Add the vegetables to the casserole. Blend the tomato paste and flour into the pan drippings in the skillet. Stir in the bouillon and $^1/_4$ cup wine gradually. Bring the mixture to a boil, stirring constantly. Add the thyme and any additional salt and pepper desired. Pour the mixture into the casserole.

Bake, covered, at 300 degrees for $1^3/_4$ to $2^1/_2$ hours or until fork-tender, stirring and adding small amounts of the remaining wine as necessary. Bake, uncovered, for 15 to 30 minutes longer, stirring frequently to avoid browning. Serve with wild rice and a green salad. Yield: 4 servings.

Approx Per Serving: Cal 567; Prot 56 g; Carbo 20 g; T Fat 25 g; 40% Calories from Fat;
Chol 157 mg; Fiber 3 g; Sod 414 mg
Nutritional information includes the entire amount of the marinade.

WINTER BEEF STEW

8 ounces bacon   2¹/₂ pounds lean beef   ¹/₄ cup flour
Salt and pepper to taste   ¹/₄ cup olive oil
3 cups chopped onions
2 garlic cloves, chopped   1¹/₂ cups orange juice   1 cup red wine
³/₄ cup tomato purée   2 beef bouillon cubes
1 teaspoon salt   ¹/₂ teaspoon pepper
¹/₄ teaspoon nutmeg   2 bay leaves
4 turnips or potatoes, peeled   5 carrots
2 tablespoons chopped parsley

Cut the bacon into small pieces. Cook the bacon in a large soup pot until crisp. Remove the bacon from the pot and set aside. Reserve the bacon drippings in the pot. Cut the beef into 2-inch cubes. Coat the beef cubes with a mixture of the flour, salt and pepper. Add the beef cubes in batches to the reserved drippings and cook over high heat until browned on all sides. Reserve the browned beef cubes. Add the olive oil to the pan drippings. Add the onions and garlic and sauté until tender.

Stir in the orange juice, wine, tomato purée, bouillon, salt, pepper, nutmeg and bay leaves. Return the beef cubes and bacon to the pot. Simmer, covered, for 30 minutes. Cut the turnips and carrots into chunks and add to the pot. Simmer, covered, for 1 hour, stirring occasionally. Remove and discard the bay leaves. Sprinkle with parsley. Serve with hot French or Italian bread.
Yield: 6 servings.

Approx Per Serving: Cal 721; Prot 46 g; Carbo 35 g; T Fat 41 g; 51% Calories from Fat;
Chol 140 mg; Fiber 6 g; Sod 1223 mg

*From the diaries of William Mordecai Hayes (born in 1840) who lived on a farm in Embreeville, halfway between Marshalton and Unionville, and was a Quaker. These diaries are in CCHS library and are unpublished. (*W.M.H.)

LAZY MAN'S CHILI

3 pounds lean ground beef
12 ounces medium-hot sausage
2 tablespoons olive oil
8 cups salsa
1 (15-ounce) can red kidney beans
1 (16-ounce) can crushed tomatoes with basil
1 envelope chili seasoning mix
3 tablespoons Worcestershire sauce
Tabasco sauce to taste

Cook the ground beef and sausage in the olive oil in a large skillet until brown and crumbly, stirring frequently. Drain the browned meat mixture and place in a large slow cooker. Stir in the salsa, undrained kidney beans, tomatoes, chili seasoning mix, Worcestershire sauce and Tabasco sauce and mix well. Cook, covered, on Medium for several hours. May adjust spiciness by choice of salsa from mild to hot. Yield: 10 servings.

Approx Per Serving: Cal 507; Prot 39 g; Carbo 26 g; T Fat 28 g; 49% Calories from Fat; Chol 112 mg; Fiber 7 g; Sod 1801 mg

6/13/1859—Clear most of the day but also cloudy and some rain. I went over after J.R. Hayes and we both went to W.C. I got a violin. Mother and Sister Allie were also in W.C. We went up and got dinner at the Turk's Head. *W.M.H.

EGGPLANT MOUSSAKA

1 medium eggplant
^{1}/4 cup (about) olive oil
1 pound ground chuck
Salt and pepper to taste
Béchamel Sauce
^{1}/2 cup grated Parmesan cheese

Slice the unpeeled eggplant into ^{1}/2-inch slices. Pour a small amount of olive oil into a large heavy skillet. Brown the eggplant slices lightly on both sides in the olive oil over medium-high heat, adding small amounts of oil as needed. Drain on paper towels and set the browned eggplant slices aside. Pour all but 1 teaspoon of the olive oil from the skillet. Add the ground chuck and cook until brown and crumbly, stirring frequently. Season the browned ground chuck with salt and pepper to taste. Alternate layers of the eggplant slices and ground chuck in a shallow 1^1/2-quart baking dish, ending with eggplant. Spoon the Béchamel Sauce over the layers. Sprinkle with the Parmesan cheese. Bake at 400 degrees for 15 to 20 minutes or until heated through and golden brown. Yield: 4 servings.

BÉCHAMEL SAUCE

2 tablespoons butter
2 tablespoons flour
1 tablespoon chopped onion
1 cup chicken bouillon
2 tablespoons heavy cream
Salt and pepper to taste

Melt the butter in a small saucepan. Add the flour and blend well. Add the onion. Stir in the bouillon gradually and cook until thickened, stirring constantly. Blend in the cream, salt and pepper. Simmer over very low heat for 15 minutes, stirring frequently. Strain if desired.

Approx Per Serving: Cal 560; Prot 33 g; Carbo 12 g; T Fat 42 g; 68% Calories from Fat;
Chol 117 mg; Fiber 4 g; Sod 560 mg

PORK TENDERLOIN DIJONAISE

2 (6-ounce) pork tenderloins
1/4 cup (about) flour
2 tablespoons butter
1 tablespoon sliced scallions
1 teaspoon minced onion or shallot
3 tablespoons white wine, chicken broth or water
31/2 ounces fresh wild mushrooms
1/4 cup heavy cream
6 tablespoons brown sauce

Remove and discard all visible fat from the tenderloins. Cut into 1-inch slices and pound with a meat mallet until very thin. Coat the tenderloin slices lightly with flour.

Preheat a large heavy skillet over medium-high heat. Add the butter. Allow the butter to melt but do not brown. Add the tenderloin slices, several at a time, and cook for not longer than 11/2 minutes on each side until golden brown. Set the tenderloin aside and keep warm.

Add the scallions and minced onion and sauté for 30 seconds. Add the wine and mushrooms. Cook for 2 minutes, stirring constantly. Add the cream and brown sauce. Bring to a boil and serve the tenderloin with the sauce immediately.

The mushrooms can be a single variety such as shiitake, oyster, portobello or cremini or a medley. Yield: 4 servings.

Approx Per Serving: Cal 294; Prot 21 g; Carbo 14 g; T Fat 16 g; 49% Calories from Fat; Chol 88 mg; Fiber 1 g; Sod 939 mg

 8/13/1859—About 9:30 John M. Stevens and I started for the Pic-Nic down Brandywine at Sager's Island and remained until 11:45 that night. Had a good time. *W.M.H.

*GRILLED PORK TENDERLOIN

Pace One Restaurant

1¹/2 cups honey
2 cups smooth Dijon mustard
3 cups vegetable oil
1¹/2 teaspoons pepper
1¹/2 teaspoons minced fresh thyme
6 (9-ounce) portions pork tenderloin
Peach Demi-Glace

Combine the honey, mustard, oil, pepper and thyme in a bowl and mix well. Trim the tenderloin and marinate in the honey-mustard mixture in the refrigerator until ready to grill. Drain the tenderloin portions and place on a grill over low heat. Grill for 20 minutes for medium to medium-well. Cut into slices and serve each portion with about 6 tablespoons Peach Demi-Glace and Stuffed Apples (page 99). Yield: 6 servings.

PEACH DEMI-GLACE

3 cups thinly sliced onions
3 tablespoons vegetable oil
¹/2 teaspoon minced fresh thyme
6 tablespoons peach brandy
¹/4 cup brandy
2¹/2 cups Pace One veal demi-glace
1¹/2 teaspoons kosher salt
¹/4 teaspoon white pepper

Caramelize the onions in the oil in a large skillet. Add the thyme and the brandies. Ignite. Cook until the mixture is reduced to ¹/4. Stir in the demi-glace. Season with the salt and pepper and simmer for 10 minutes. Strain and keep warm.

Approx Per Serving: Cal 1771; Prot 60 g; Carbo 84 g; T Fat 132 g; 65% Calories from Fat;
Chol 151 mg; Fiber 2 g; Sod 2603 mg
Nutritional information includes the entire amount of the marinade, but does not
include the Pace One Veal demi-glace.

MAKE-AHEAD SAUSAGE AND EGG CASSEROLE

12 ounces mild Italian sausage
2 (8-ounce) cartons egg substitute
1 cup skim milk
$1/4$ teaspoon salt
$3/4$ teaspoon Dijon mustard
$1/4$ cup shredded Cheddar cheese
3 green onions, chopped
6 slices white bread

Remove the casings from the sausage. Cook the sausage in a skillet until cooked through and brown on all sides. Drain in a colander and pat with paper towels to drain well. Crumble the sausage and set aside.

Beat the egg substitute with the skim milk in a large bowl. Add the salt and mustard and beat until well blended. Add the Cheddar cheese and green onions and mix well. Cut the bread slices into $1/2$-inch cubes. Add the bread cubes and sausage to the egg mixture and stir just until mixed.

Pour the mixture into a 7×11-inch baking dish sprayed with nonstick cooking spray. Chill, covered, for 8 to 12 hours. Bake, uncovered, at 350 degrees for 50 minutes or until set and lightly browned. Garnish with cherry tomatoes and chopped green onion tops. Yield: 6 servings.

Approx Per Serving: Cal 342; Prot 20 g; Carbo 22 g; T Fat 19 g; 50% Calories from Fat;
Chol 31 mg; Fiber 1 g; Sod 744 mg

Lamb

LEG OF LAMB CHESTER COUNTY-STYLE

1 (8-pound) leg of lamb, bone-in
2 garlic cloves, chopped
1½ teaspoons salt
Pepper to taste
1 bay leaf, crushed
½ teaspoon sage
1 teaspoon ginger
½ teaspoon marjoram
1 teaspoon soy sauce
2 teaspoons olive oil
Dash of Soul Food seasoning

Trim any excess fat from the lamb and pierce the lamb all over with a fork or sharp knife. Combine the garlic, salt, pepper, bay leaf, sage, ginger, marjoram, soy sauce, olive oil and seasoning in a small bowl and mix well. Spread the mixture over the lamb and place the lamb on a rack in a roasting pan. Place in a preheated 425-degree oven. Roast for 25 minutes. Reduce the temperature to 325 degrees. Roast until a meat thermometer reaches 130 degrees for medium or 145 degrees for well done. Let stand for 20 minutes before slicing. Yield: 6 servings.

Approx Per Serving: Cal 467; Prot 63 g; Carbo <1 g; T Fat 22 g; 44% Calories from Fat;
Chol 204 mg; Fiber <1 g; Sod 812 mg

 2/20/1860 (Mon.)—Took the borrowed sleigh home, went to Unionville and to West Chester. Saw the big ox. In the evening we went to a party at Mortonville. . . . Taylor's Band played. There were sixty to seventy couples. *W.M.H.

LAMB DIVINE

1 (7-pound) leg of lamb, butterflied
20 garlic cloves   3 sprigs rosemary   Sea salt to taste
1/2 cup Dijon mustard

Place the lamb on a work surface. Crush the garlic using a mortar and pestle or food processor. Strip the rosemary leaves from the stems, mince and mix with the garlic. Add the sea salt. Reserve a portion of the garlic mixture and spread the remaining mixture on the lamb. Roll the lamb up and tie securely. Spread the reserved garlic mixture and the mustard over the lamb. Place on a rack in a roasting pan. Roast at 375 degrees for 25 minutes per pound. Let rest for several minutes before slicing. Yield: 6 servings.

Approx Per Serving: Cal 430; Prot 56 g; Carbo 3 g; T Fat 20 g; 43% Calories from Fat;
Chol 178 mg; Fiber <1 g; Sod 643 mg

A SHEPHERD'S PIE

2 pounds lamb, pork or beef cubes
Curry powder to taste   Garlic powder to taste
2 tablespoons (about) olive oil
2 large onions, sliced   4 carrots, chopped
3 cups green beans
1 (10-ounce) can cream of mushroom soup
2 cups mashed potatoes
3/4 teaspoon minced parsley

Sprinkle the lamb with curry powder and garlic powder. Brown the lamb in the olive oil in a large heavy skillet over medium-high heat and set aside. Layer the onions, carrots, green beans, browned lamb cubes and soup in a casserole. Bake, covered, at 350 degrees for 1 1/2 hours. Spread the potatoes over the top and sprinkle with the parsley. Bake, uncovered, for 30 minutes.
Yield: 8 servings.

Approx Per Serving: Cal 309; Prot 22 g; Carbo 22 g; T Fat 15 g; 43% Calories from Fat;
Chol 69 mg; Fiber 4 g; Sod 492 mg

SHEPHERD'S PIE WITH SMASHED POTATOES

2 medium onions, finely chopped
3 tablespoons chopped garlic
1 rib celery, finely chopped
2 tablespoons olive oil   5 pounds ground lamb
3 medium carrots, finely chopped
2 tablespoons chopped rosemary
1/2 cup madeira wine*
1 cup tomato paste
2 tablespoons beef base   Salt and pepper to taste
Smashed Potatoes

*Famed as the favorite wine of Thomas Jefferson and
others during colonial times.

Sauté the onions, garlic and celery in the oil in a large skillet over medium-high heat just until tender. Add the lamb, carrots, rosemary and wine and cook until the lamb is crumbly and the carrots tender, stirring frequently. Add the tomato paste, beef base, salt and pepper and mix well. Reduce the heat and simmer for several minutes. Divide the Smashed Potatoes among 6 dinner plates and spoon the lamb mixture over the top. Yield: 6 servings.

SMASHED POTATOES

4 large baking potatoes
2 quarts water
Garlic salt and pepper to taste
1/2 cup butter

Scrub the potatoes well. Cut the unpeeled potatoes into small pieces. Bring the water to a boil in a large saucepan. Add the potatoes and cook for about 10 minutes or until tender. Drain the potatoes and smash slightly in a mixing bowl. Add the garlic salt, pepper and butter and fold until well mixed.

Approx Per Serving: Cal 1187; Prot 72 g; Carbo 53 g; T Fat 74 g; 56% Calories from Fat;
Chol 292 mg; Fiber 7 g; Sod 2063 mg

VENISON MARINADE

1¹/₂ cups red wine
6 tablespoons soy sauce
1¹/₂ tablespoons Dijon mustard
1 tablespoon chopped garlic
1 tablespoon crushed peppercorns
2 pounds venison

Combine the wine, soy sauce, mustard, garlic and peppercorns in a large sealable plastic bag. Add the venison, squeeze the air from the bag and seal tightly. Marinate the venison in the refrigerator for 1 to 3 days. Drain and cook the venison in your favorite recipe. Yield: 1 recipe.

Approx Per Recipe: Cal 1785; Prot 209 g; Carbo 22 g; T Fat 66 g; 34% Calories from Fat;
Chol 730 mg; Fiber <1 g; Sod 10851 mg
Nutritional information includes the entire amount of the marinade and venison.

*MOTHER'S BOHEMPEN DUCK

1 duck
Marjoram to taste
Salt to taste

Rinse the duck and pat dry. Rub the duck cavity with a mixture of marjoram and salt. Prick the duck skin all over with particular attention to all the fat pockets, especially around the legs and thighs. Place the duck on a rack in a roasting pan. Roast at 375 degrees for 2¹/₂ hours, pricking the fat pockets about every 30 minutes. The skin will have the consistency of potato chips when the duck is ready. Yield: 4 servings.

Approx Per Serving: Cal 644; Prot 36 g; Carbo 0 g; T Fat 54 g; 77% Calories from Fat;
Chol 160 mg; Fiber 0 g; Sod 113 mg

CHICKEN AND GROUNDNUT STEW

9 chicken thighs, skinned
2 tablespoons olive oil
2 medium onions, chopped
2 garlic cloves, minced
1 teaspoon curry powder
$1/2$ teaspoon dried thyme
2 bay leaves
$1/2$ teaspoon salt
$1/4$ teaspoon cayenne pepper
3 cups chicken broth
1 (16-ounce) jar spaghetti sauce
$3/4$ cup creamy peanut butter

Cook the chicken thighs in the olive oil in a Dutch oven over medium-high heat for about 6 minutes or until browned on all sides. Remove the chicken and set aside. Add the onions and cook for about 5 minutes, stirring frequently.

Add the garlic, curry powder, thyme, bay leaves, salt and cayenne pepper and cook for 1 minute, stirring constantly. Add the broth and spaghetti sauce and mix well. Return the chicken to the Dutch oven and reduce the heat.

Simmer, covered, for 45 minutes or until the chicken is cooked through. Place about 1 cup of the hot sauce in a bowl. Add the peanut butter and whisk until well blended. Stir the peanut butter mixture into the chicken. Cook for 2 minutes or until heated to serving temperature. Serve over hot cooked rice or noodles.

Peanut butter stews abound all over the African continent. Their spiciness ranges from five-alarm to a warm glow, and this stew falls in between. I serve this during my Kwanzaa celebrations. Yield: 6 servings.

Approx Per Serving: Cal 510; Prot 33 g; Carbo 22 g; T Fat 34 g; 58% Calories from Fat;
Chol 74 mg; Fiber 5 g; Sod 1176 mg

SAVORY CHICKEN STIR-FRY

4 ounces baby portobello mushrooms
4 ounces white mushrooms
1 large onion $1^1/_2$ large carrots $1^1/_2$ ribs celery
$1/_2$ green bell pepper $1/_2$ orange bell pepper
3 tablespoons (about) canola oil
8 small or 4 large garlic cloves
1 cup ($1/_4$-inch strips) chicken, beef or pork
20 to 30 grinds coarse black pepper   Salt to taste
6 tablespoons white wine for chicken or pork or red wine for beef
6 tablespoons orange juice
6 tablespoons mango or papaya juice or jelly
4 to 6 tablespoons duck sauce
1 tablespoon balsamic vinegar   1 teaspoon ground ginger
1 (14-ounce) can chicken or beef broth
3 tablespoons soy sauce   2 tablespoons cornstarch
$1/_2$ cup snow peas $1^1/_2$ cups cooked rice

Prepare all the vegetables but keep separate. Chop the mushrooms and onion coarsely. Slice the carrots, celery and bell peppers into $1/_4$-inch strips. Heat enough oil in a heavy 14-inch skillet over medium-high to high heat to cover the bottom of the skillet with $1/_8$ inch of the oil. Press the garlic into the hot oil and stir-fry until golden. Add the chicken gradually, stir-frying and pushing the cooked chicken to the side of the skillet. Add pepper and salt little by little as the ingredients are added to the skillet. Add the mushrooms. Stir-fry until almost brown and push to the side of the skillet. Add the onion. Stir-fry until brown and push to the side of the skillet. Add the carrots, celery and bell peppers. Stir-fry until light brown and push to the side of the skillet.

Add the wine to the skillet and stir to deglaze the bottom of the skillet. Add the fruit juices, duck sauce, vinegar and ginger and mix well. Reduce the heat and bring to a simmer. Combine the broth, soy sauce and cornstarch in a jar, cover and shake vigorously to mix. Stir into the skillet. Cook until thickened, stirring constantly. Add the snow peas. Simmer until the vegetables are tender. Serve over the rice. Do not substitute grape jelly for the mango or papaya juice or jelly. Yield: 4 servings.

Approx Per Serving: Cal 434; Prot 21 g; Carbo 52 g; T Fat 14 g; 30% Calories from Fat;
Chol 32 mg; Fiber 4 g; Sod 1770 mg

STUFFED CORNISH HENS WITH BURGUNDY SAUCE

2 (1-pound) Cornish hens
Salt and pepper to taste
3 tablespoons sliced green onions
3 tablespoons butter
3 tablespoons chopped parsley
6 tablespoons slivered almonds
$1/2$ cup cooked wild rice
Burgundy Sauce

Rinse the hens and pat dry. Season inside and out with salt and pepper. Sauté the green onions in the butter in a small skillet until wilted. Combine with the parsley, almonds and wild rice in a mixing bowl and toss to mix. Adjust the seasonings and stuff the hens. Place the stuffed hens in a baking dish. Spoon the Burgundy Sauce over the hens. Roast at 350 degrees for 40 minutes, basting frequently. Sprinkle with a small amount of additional burgundy. Roast for 5 minutes longer. Serve with a sparkling burgundy. Yield: 2 servings.

BURGUNDY SAUCE

$1/2$ cup currant jelly
2 tablespoons butter
4 teaspoons lemon juice
2 teaspoons cornstarch
2 teaspoons Worcestershire sauce
$1/2$ teaspoon allspice
$1/4$ cup sparkling burgundy

Heat the jelly and butter in a small saucepan until melted. Blend the lemon juice and cornstarch in a small bowl. Add the Worcestershire sauce, allspice and burgundy and mix well. Stir the mixture into the melted jelly mixture and bring to a boil, stirring constantly.

Approx Per Serving: Cal 1254; Prot 70 g; Carbo 82 g; T Fat 73 g; 51% Calories from Fat; Chol 276 mg; Fiber 4 g; Sod 1074 mg

CILANTRO- AND BASIL-STUFFED TURKEY BREAST

1 (4-pound) boneless skinless turkey breast
Salt and pepper to taste   2 tablespoons butter
3 tablespoons water   ³/4 cup shredded cabbage
1¹/4 cup finely chopped peeled potato
¹/4 cup finely chopped broccoli florets
¹/2 cup shredded carrot   ¹/4 cup finely chopped celery
¹/3 cup finely chopped red bell pepper
³/4 cup finely chopped onion
1¹/2 teaspoons minced cilantro or parsley
1 tablespoon chopped fresh basil
1¹/2 cups water   2 tablespoons flour
3 tablespoons water

Place the turkey breast on waxed paper. Slice the turkey breast horizontally to, but not through, the thickest part to butterfly. Lay the turkey open and cover with waxed paper. Flatten into a rectangle with a uniform thickness with a rolling pin or meat mallet. Discard the waxed paper, blot the turkey with paper towels and sprinkle with salt and pepper on both sides; set aside. Melt the butter in a skillet. Add 3 tablespoons water, all the vegetables, salt and pepper to taste and mix well. Cook over low heat for 15 minutes or until the vegetables are tender but not brown, stirring occasionally. Remove the vegetables to paper towels and blot to remove excess moisture. Spread the vegetable mixture evenly over the turkey and sprinkle with the cilantro and basil. Roll the turkey and filling as for a jelly roll and tie with string in several places to secure. Place the turkey roll in a roasting pan and add 1¹/2 cups water. Sprinkle the turkey lightly with salt.

Bake, covered, at 325 degrees for 1¹/2 hours, basting occasionally. Remove the turkey to a serving platter. Let stand for 15 minutes or longer before slicing. Blend the flour with 3 tablespoons water. Bring the pan juices to a simmer and stir in the flour mixture gradually. Cook just until the mixture comes to a boil and is slightly thickened, stirring constantly. Serve a slice of the turkey roll on a mixture of brown and wild rice with gravy drizzled over the top. Surround with seasoned broccoli and dilled carrots and green beans garnished with minced parsley. Yield: 4 servings.

Approx Per Serving: Cal 662; Prot 121 g; Carbo 18 g; T Fat 9 g; 13% Calories from Fat;
Chol 343 mg; Fiber 3 g; Sod 284 mg

PASTA WITH CLAM SAUCE

3 garlic cloves, minced
1/2 cup olive oil   3 (6-ounce) cans minced clams
Salt and pepper to taste
2 tablespoons butter   1 large tomato, chopped
8 ounces angel hair pasta
Grated Parmesan cheese to taste   Freshly ground pepper to taste

Sauté the garlic in the olive oil in a large skillet. Drain the clams, reserving the liquid. Add the clams to the skillet. Cook over low heat for 10 minutes, stirring occasionally. Add salt and pepper, butter, tomato and the reserved clam liquid. Simmer, covered, for 10 minutes. Cook the pasta according to the package directions; drain but do not rinse. Divide the hot pasta among 3 dinner plates or pasta bowls, sprinkle with Parmesan cheese, ladle the sauce over the pasta and add a sprinkle of freshly ground pepper. Yield: 3 servings.

Approx Per Serving: Cal 754; Prot 34 g; Carbo 50 g; T Fat 47 g; 56% Calories from Fat;
Chol 81 mg; Fiber 2 g; Sod 613 mg

CRAB WITH CAPERS CASSEROLE

1 pound crab meat, flaked   1 1/2 teaspoons minced onion
1/2 cup reduced-fat mayonnaise
1 teaspoon white wine Worcestershire sauce
2 tablespoons white wine   1 teaspoon Old Bay seasoning
Juice of 1/2 lemon
2 tablespoons drained capers   1/2 cup fine dry bread crumbs
1 tablespoon melted butter

Combine the crab meat, onion, mayonnaise, Worcestershire sauce, wine, seasoning, lemon juice and capers in a mixing bowl and mix well. Spoon the mixture into a greased 2-quart casserole. Toss the bread crumbs with the melted butter and sprinkle over the top. Dust with additional Old Bay seasoning. Bake at 375 degrees for 30 minutes. Yield: 4 servings.

Approx Per Serving: Cal 273; Prot 25 g; Carbo 17 g; T Fat 11 g; 36% Calories from Fat;
Chol 95 mg; Fiber <1 g; Sod 1030 mg

FRAGILE CRAB CAKES WITH BEURRE BLANC

1 small onion, finely chopped
1 medium red bell pepper, finely chopped
2 tablespoons butter
8 ounces lump crab meat, flaked
3/4 cup bread crumbs
2 eggs
1 teaspoon Dijon mustard
1 teaspoon prepared horseradish
1/4 cup minced cilantro or parsley
1 tablespoon butter
1 tablespoon vegetable oil
Beurre Blanc

Sauté the onion and red pepper in 2 tablespoons butter in a skillet until tender. Combine with the crab meat and bread crumbs in a mixing bowl. Beat the eggs with the mustard and horseradish and add to the crab meat mixture. Add the cilantro and mix well. Shape into 6 patties. Chill, covered with plastic wrap, for 1 hour. Heat 1 tablespoon butter with the oil in a skillet. Fry the crab cakes for 3 minutes on each side. Serve the crab cakes with Beurre Blanc. Yield: 6 servings.

BEURRE BLANC

1 shallot, finely chopped
1/4 cup white wine
Juice of 1/2 lemon
1/2 cup (1 stick) cold butter
Salt and pepper to taste

Combine the shallot and wine in a small skillet. Bring to a boil and boil until almost dry. Remove from the heat and add the lemon juice. Cut the butter into 4 portions. Add the butter 1 portion at a time to the shallot mixture and whisk until the butter melts. Return to the heat. Heat to serving temperature but do not allow to come to a simmer. Season with salt and pepper.

Approx Per Serving: Cal 345; Prot 12 g; Carbo 1 g; T Fat 26 g; 68% Calories from Fat; Chol 155 mg; Fiber 1 g; Sod 511 mg

CRAWFISH CAKES

The Ship Inn

1 pound shelled crawfish tails
2 small scallions, chopped
1 medium roasted red pepper, chopped
2 tablespoons chopped fresh parsley
1 egg   ³/₄ cup mayonnaise
¹/₂ teaspoon Old Bay seasoning
Salt and pepper to taste
1 tablespoon (or more) dry bread crumbs
Vegetable oil for frying

Drain the crawfish, reserve several of the tails to keep whole and coarsely chop the remaining crawfish. Combine the whole and chopped crawfish with the scallions and roasted pepper in a mixing bowl. Add the parsley, egg, mayonnaise, seasonings and enough bread crumbs to make the mixture of the desired consistency. Shape the mixture into cakes of the desired size. Heat the vegetable oil in a large skillet. Brown the crawfish cakes for 1 minute on each side. If the cakes are large, it may be necessary to place them on a baking sheet and bake at 350 degrees for 12 to 15 minutes. Yield: 4 servings.

Approx Per Serving: Cal 407; Prot 17 g; Carbo 3 g; T Fat 36 g; 80% Calories from Fat;
Chol 204 mg; Fiber <1 g; Sod 478 mg
The nutritional information does not include the oil for frying.

8/23/1860—Clear and pleasant. I had but few scholars today owing to the Camp Meeting attractions. I went to Camp in the evening about 2¹/₂ miles from here. (Embreeville) *W.M.H.

Note: *The Camp-Meeting, usually Methodist-inspired, was an "enthusiastic" institution. They were held annually in a particular district. People would come from 50–100 miles for services that were held over a number of days—usually AFTER harvest. These gatherings were religious, social and sexual. "More souls were probably conceived than saved."*

People of other religious convictions, such as Quakers, looked upon Camp Meetings as a social function, a type of entertainment.

PASTA WITH SALMON AND ASPARAGUS

1 pound linguini   4 ounces smoked salmon
1 cup minced fresh asparagus
1/4 cup butter   2 tablespoons chopped fresh parsley
1 cup cream   1 tablespoon flour
1/2 cup grated Jarlsberg cheese
Freshly ground black pepper to taste

Cook the linguini according to the package directions, drain, rinse with cold water, drain well and set aside. Flake the salmon. Stir-fry the salmon and asparagus in the butter in a skillet. Add the parsley and cream and mix gently. Bring to a simmer over low heat. Simmer for 5 minutes. Whisk in the flour. Divide the cooled pasta among 6 plates. Ladle the sauce over the pasta and sprinkle with the cheese and pepper. Yield: 6 servings.

Approx Per Serving: Cal 553; Prot 17 g; Carbo 60 g; T Fat 27 g; 44% Calories from Fat; Chol 8 mg; Fiber 2 g; Sod 272 mg

CREAMY DILLED SALMON

4 (6-ounce) salmon fillets
Salt and freshly ground pepper to taste
2 tablespoons butter   2 to 3 teaspoons minced fresh dill
1 tablespoon lemon juice   1/4 cup heavy cream

Rinse the salmon, pat dry and season with salt and pepper. Place the butter in a 9-inch microwave-safe baking dish. Microwave on High for 45 seconds or until melted. Stir in the dill and lemon juice. Arrange the salmon in the dish, turning to coat both sides. Microwave, covered with plastic wrap, on High for 3 to 6 minutes or until the salmon is opaque. Remove the salmon to a serving plate and cover with foil. Blend the cream into the salmon juices. Microwave on Medium until thickened. Adjust the seasonings. Spoon over the salmon. Garnish with dill or parsley sprigs. Yield: 4 servings.

Approx Per Serving: Cal 356; Prot 32 g; Carbo 1 g; T Fat 24 g; 62% Calories from Fat; Chol 138 mg; Fiber <1 g; Sod 142 mg

SALMON IN PUFF PASTRY

Provence Restaurant and Wine Bar

2 (6-inch) squares puff pastry
1 (5-ounce) portion boned, skinned salmon
2 teaspoons Herbs of Provence (see page 17)
Salt and pepper to taste
2 tablespoons soft goat cheese
Spinach Crème

Roll each piece of puff pastry approximately 1 inch bigger on all sides than the salmon piece. Place the salmon on one of the pastry squares. Sprinkle with the herbs, salt and pepper and press the goat cheese gently on top. Cover with the remaining puff pastry, trim the pastry with a sharp knife if necessary and press the top and bottom pastries together with a fork to seal. Place on a nonstick baking sheet. Bake at 400 degrees for 10 to 12 minutes or until golden brown. Cover with foil and bake for 5 minutes longer for well-cooked salmon. Spoon the Spinach Crème onto the center of a warm plate. Cut the hot salmon in pastry diagonally with a serrated knife. Place half the salmon in the center of the plate and top with the remaining half. Serve immediately. Yield: 1 serving.

SPINACH CRÈME

15 spinach leaves
1 tablespoon olive oil
2 cups heavy cream
$1/8$ teaspoon nutmeg
Salt and pepper to taste
1 tablespoon Pernod liqueur

Sauté the spinach in the hot olive oil in a sauté pan for several seconds until lightly wilted but not brown. Set aside. Bring the cream to a simmer in a small saucepan. Add the spinach, nutmeg, salt and pepper. Cook over low heat until thickened, stirring frequently. Add the Pernod liqueur.

Approx Per Serving: Cal 2538; Prot 52 g; Carbo 71 g; T Fat 229 g; 80% Calories from Fat; Chol 751 mg; Fiber 10 g; Sod 746 mg

SALMON WELLINGTON

3 tablespoons butter, melted
1 (8-ounce) can artichoke bottoms, drained, chopped
1 onion, chopped   1 pound mushrooms, chopped
1/4 cup madeira   Salt and pepper to taste   Cream Cheese Pastry
8 (6-ounce) salmon fillets   1 egg yolk
1 tablespoon milk   White Wine Sauce

Combine the butter, artichokes, onion, mushrooms, wine, salt and pepper in a skillet and mix well. Cook over low heat for 10 minutes, stirring frequently. Refrigerate, covered, until chilled or for up to 2 days. Roll the Cream Cheese Pastry on a lightly floured surface and cut into 8 rectangles large enough to cover the top of the salmon. Place the salmon fillets on a lightly greased baking sheet. Top each with a spoonful of the artichoke mixture, place Pastry over the top and tuck under. Beat the egg yolk with the milk and brush over the pastry. Bake at 425 degrees for 20 to 25 minutes or until golden brown. Serve with the White Wine Sauce. Yield: 8 servings.

CREAM CHEESE PASTRY

1 cup (2 sticks) cold butter   8 ounces cream cheese, chilled
2 cups flour

Cut the butter and cream cheese into pieces, place in a food processor and process until well blended. Add the flour and process until blended. Shape the dough into 2 flat balls, wrap in plastic wrap and chill for several hours to 1 week. (Freeze for longer storage.)

WHITE WINE SAUCE

6 tablespoons dry white wine   6 tablespoons white wine vinegar
2 tablespoons minced onion
1 1/2 cups heavy cream, at room temperature
1/4 teaspoon salt   White pepper to taste   2 tablespoons chopped chives

Combine all the ingredients in a small saucepan. Simmer for 5 minutes, stirring frequently.

Approx Per Serving: Cal 927; Prot 42 g; Carbo 33 g; T Fat 68 g; 66% Calories from Fat;
Chol 295 mg; Fiber 2 g; Sod 617 mg

PAN-SEARED SEA SCALLOPS

The Dilworthtown Inn

3 Diver scallops   Salt and pepper to taste
2 tablespoons olive oil or clarified butter   Nage   Potato Croquettes

Preheat a heavy skillet until smoking. Sprinkle the scallops with salt and pepper. Add the olive oil to the hot skillet and place the scallops in the hot olive oil. Cook until lightly browned on both sides. Spoon the Nage sauce in the center of a plate and add the scallops, Potato Croquettes and vegetables. Yield: 1 serving.

NAGE

2 quarts vegetable or lobster stock   3 asparagus spears
Kernels from 1 ear of corn   1 quart heavy cream
Salt and pepper to taste   Asparagus tips
Fresh tarragon leaves   Corn kernels
Finely chopped red and yellow bell peppers   Chopped scallions

Combine the stock, asparagus spears, corn and cream in large saucepan. Simmer until thickened to the desired consistency, stirring and skimming occasionally; strain. Pour the desired amount of the sauce into a sauté pan. Add the desired amounts of vegetables. Bring to a boil.

POTATO CROQUETTES

1 pound purple Yukon potatoes, scrubbed, cut up $1/2$ cup butter
$3/4$ cup milk $1/2$ cup chopped scallions
Salt and pepper to taste $1/2$ cup flour   2 eggs, beaten
1 cup dry bread crumbs   Vegetable oil for deep-frying

Cook the potatoes in boiling water to cover until tender, drain and put through a ricer. Beat in the butter, milk, scallions, salt and pepper. Cool. Shape by $1 1/2$ to 2 ounces of the mixture into rounds and roll in the flour. Dip the croquettes into the eggs and roll in the bread crumbs. Place the croquettes on a parchment paper-lined tray. Refrigerate for 1 hour. Deep-fry until golden brown.

The nutritional information for this recipe is not available.

CURRIED SHRIMP CASSEROLE

1 (6-ounce) package curried rice
1¹/2 pounds unpeeled shrimp
2 ribs celery, chopped
1 onion, chopped
3 garlic cloves, minced
¹/4 cup butter
¹/2 cup tomato sauce
1 cup half-and-half
¹/2 teaspoon cayenne pepper
Hot sauce to taste
2 cups shredded Cheddar cheese
1 bay leaf

Prepare the rice according to the package directions and let stand until cool. Cook the shrimp in boiling water just until the shrimp turn pink. Peel and devein when cool.

Sauté the celery, onion and garlic in the butter in a skillet until tender. Mix the tomato sauce, half-and-half, cayenne pepper and hot sauce together.

Combine the rice, shrimp, sautéed vegetables and tomato sauce mixture in a mixing bowl and mix well. Add half the Cheddar cheese and mix well. Spoon into a greased 2-quart casserole. Place the bay leaf on top. Refrigerate, covered, for 24 hours or freeze for later.

Bake, uncovered, at 400 degrees for 30 minutes. Remove and discard the bay leaf. Top with the remaining cheese. Bake for 5 minutes longer or until the cheese is melted. Yield: 6 servings.

Approx Per Serving: Cal 454; Prot 28 g; Carbo 28 g; T Fat 26 g; 51% Calories from Fat;
Chol 210 mg; Fiber 2 g; Sod 931 mg

 12/14/1860—Sister Allie and I went to Joshua Pierce's for supper and afterward the Lyceum in the evening. The question for debate—Should women have equal political rights with men? *W.M.H.

SHRIMP AND PASTA SALSA CASSEROLE

2 eggs   1 cup milk   1 cup plain yogurt
4 ounces Swiss cheese, shredded   1/3 cup crumbled feta cheese
1/3 cup chopped fresh parsley
1/4 cup chopped fresh basil, or 2 teaspoons dried basil
1 teaspoon crushed dried oregano leaves
1 (9-ounce) package fresh angel hair pasta
1 (16-ounce) jar medium-hot thick and chunky salsa
1 pound peeled medium shrimp, deveined
1 cup shredded Monterey Jack cheese

Beat the eggs in a mixing bowl. Add the milk, yogurt, Swiss cheese, feta cheese, parsley, basil and oregano and mix well. Spread half the uncooked pasta in a greased 9×13-inch baking pan. Cover with the salsa and add a layer of half the shrimp. Add layers of the remaining pasta, the egg mixture and the remaining shrimp. Sprinkle with the Monterey Jack cheese. Bake at 350 degrees for 40 minutes. Yield: 6 servings.

Approx Per Serving: Cal 440; Prot 33 g; Carbo 36 g; T Fat 18 g; 38% Calories from Fat;
Chol 231 mg; Fiber 1 g; Sod 1092 mg

*SHRIMP WITH PERNOD

1 1/2 pounds unpeeled shrimp   3 tablespoons butter
2 tablespoons finely chopped shallots
2 tablespoons Pernod liqueur   1 cup heavy cream
Salt and freshly ground pepper to taste

Peel and devein the shrimp. Melt the butter in a skillet. Add the shrimp and shallots. Sauté for 3 to 4 minutes or just until the shrimp turn pink. Add the Pernod liqueur. Remove the shrimp with a slotted spoon. Stir in the cream. Cook over high heat for 1 minute, stirring constantly. Add salt and pepper and return the shrimp to the skillet. Heat to serving temperature. Serve over hot cooked rice. Yield: 4 servings.

Approx Per Serving: Cal 413; Prot 23 g; Carbo 6 g; T Fat 32 g; 69% Calories from Fat;
Chol 307 mg; Fiber <1 g; Sod 343 mg

MUSHROOM FLORENTINE

4 portobello mushrooms
1 tablespoon (about) olive oil
Old Bay seasoning to taste
1 (10-ounce) package frozen creamed spinach, thawed
1 cup shredded sharp Cheddar cheese
1 roasted red pepper

Remove the stems from the mushrooms and discard or reserve for another purpose. Brush the mushroom caps with the olive oil, sprinkle with the seasoning and place stem side down on a broiler pan. Broil for 6 to 10 minutes or until brown.

Turn the mushrooms over and fill with the creamed spinach. Sprinkle with the Cheddar cheese. Cut the roasted red pepper into strips and arrange on top. Broil until the cheese is melted. Serve as a main course, side dish or appetizer. Yield: 4 servings.

Approx Per Serving: Cal 293; Prot 17 g; Carbo 16 g; T Fat 20 g; 59% Calories from Fat;
Chol 30 mg; Fiber 8 g; Sod 678 mg

1/9/1862 (Thurs.)—About three o'clock sisters and I started for Paxson Vickers' to attend the "Home-coming" of John and Sallie (*Vickers*) Oberholtzen. We took tea at Vickers' and then, accompanied by Paxson and Ann, we went over to Elias Oberholtzen's (*in Lionville*). There were some seventy-five people there, only a few we knew however.
    We returned to Vickers' and remained all night. *W.M.H.

PORTOBELLO SALAD

1 pound portobello mushrooms
²/₃ cup Italian salad dressing
1 (10-ounce) package spinach
8 ounces feta cheese, crumbled
3 plum tomatoes, sliced
¹/₃ cup thinly sliced red onion
¹/₃ cup Italian salad dressing

Place the mushrooms in a shallow dish. Pour ²/₃ cup salad dressing over the mushrooms, turning to coat. Marinate in the refrigerator for 1 hour, turning frequently. Drain the mushrooms. Grill or broil for 8 to 10 minutes or until cooked through, turning as necessary. Cut the mushrooms into slices. Rinse the spinach and pat dry. Tear the spinach into bite-size pieces and place in a salad bowl. Add the mushrooms, feta cheese, tomatoes and red onion and toss lightly to mix. Add ¹/₃ cup salad dressing and toss lightly. Serve immediately. Yield: 4 servings.

Approx Per Serving: Cal 480; Prot 15 g; Carbo 19 g; T Fat 41 g; 73% Calories from Fat;
Chol 50 mg; Fiber 7 g; Sod 1169 mg

1/10/1862—We all went back to Oberholtzens' for dinner. . . . After partaking a good supper of turkey and oysters we participated in the dance. *W.M.H.

POLENTA RUSTICA TORTE

Vickers Tavern

2 cups yellow cornmeal   6 cups boiling water
1 tablespoon chopped garlic $^1/_2$ cup chopped sun-dried tomato
1 tablespoon chopped basil $^3/_4$ cup grated Parmesan cheese
3 portobello mushrooms   1 medium zucchini
2 red bell peppers   Salt and pepper to taste
8 ounces mozzarella cheese, sliced
4 ounces asiago cheese, sliced

Stir the cornmeal gradually into the boiling water in a large saucepan. Add the garlic, sun-dried tomato, basil and Parmesan cheese, mixing well. Simmer for 5 to 8 minutes, stirring frequently. Grill the mushrooms and zucchini until tender. Roast the red peppers until the skins char. Peel the peppers and cut the peppers and grilled mushrooms into strips. Slice the zucchini. Spray a 9-inch springform pan with nonstick cooking spray. Spread the cornmeal mixture evenly in the pan. Sprinkle each layer lightly with salt and pepper. Arrange the zucchini slices over the cornmeal layer and add a layer of half the mozzarella and asiago cheese slices. Add layers of the red pepper strips and the remaining cheese slices. Arrange the mushroom slices over the top. Bake at 400 degrees for 30 minutes. Loosen from the side of the pan and remove the side of the pan. Slice the torte as for a cake and serve on a bed of tomato sauce or pesto sauce. May add layers of about 4 ounces shaved prosciutto with the cheese if desired. Yield: 8 servings.

Approx Per Serving: Cal 336; Prot 20 g; Carbo 35 g; T Fat 14 g; 37% Calories from Fat;
Chol 43 mg; Fiber 7 g; Sod 344 mg

 2/6/1862 (Thurs.)—After tea, I went back to Unionville and took Marietta Chandler to a ball at the Boro Hall, Kennett Square. The ball was for the benefit of the soldiers. Everything was in fine style and I enjoyed myself <u>extremely much</u>. *W.M.H.

PASTA AND POTATOES

1 or 2 large baking potatoes
1 cup olive oil
8 to 12 garlic cloves, coarsely chopped
1 dried hot pepper, chopped
12 ounces pasta, such as spaghetti, linguini or capellini
Salt and freshly ground pepper to taste
$1/4$ to $1/2$ cup chopped fresh parsley

Scrub the potatoes and prick with a fork. Bake at 400 degrees for 40 minutes or until almost tender. Let stand until cool enough to handle. Cut into $1/4$- to $1/2$-inch slices. Heat the olive oil in a large saucepan. Add the garlic, hot pepper and potato slices. Cook over medium heat for 5 minutes or until the potatoes are golden, stirring frequently.

Cook the pasta al dente, drain well and add to the potato mixture, tossing to mix. Season with salt and pepper. Divide among 4 pasta bowls and sprinkle with the parsley. Serve with salad and bread. Yield: 4 servings.

Approx Per Serving: Cal 910; Prot 14 g; Carbo 90 g; T Fat 56 g; 55% Calories from Fat;
Chol 0 mg; Fiber 5 g; Sod 19 mg

4/15/1862—After dinner went to James Pyles' and engaged Lou Pyle to go to a party at Lamborn's near Unionville next sixth day night. General Beauregard of Southern Confederacy is reported as dead in today's paper—from having his arm shot off in the battle last First day week. *W.M.H.

Note: *Beauregard did lose his arm but not his life.*

PIEROGI CASSEROLE

9 lasagna noodles
8 medium potatoes
$^1/_4$ cup butter
$^1/_2$ cup (about) milk
$1^1/_2$ cups shredded sharp Cheddar cheese
Salt and pepper to taste
2 large onions, sliced
$^1/_2$ cup butter
$^1/_2$ cup grated Parmesan cheese

Prepare the lasagna noodles according to package directions; drain. Peel the potatoes and cut into chunks. Cook the potatoes in water to cover in a saucepan until tender and drain well. Add $^1/_4$ cup butter, milk, Cheddar cheese, salt and pepper and mash until well mixed. Sauté the onions in $^1/_2$ cup butter in a skillet until tender.

Place a layer of about $^2/_3$ of the sautéed onions in a 9×13-inch baking dish. Add layers of half the lasagna noodles, all the mashed potatoes, remaining onions and remaining noodles. Sprinkle the Parmesan cheese over the top. Bake, covered with foil, at 350 degrees for 45 minutes.
Yield: 6 servings.

Approx Per Serving: Cal 565; Prot 17 g; Carbo 45 g; T Fat 36 g; 57% Calories from Fat;
Chol 101 mg; Fiber 4 g; Sod 586 mg

 6/9/1863—We had five in the office both yesterday and today. R. Davis had a bad cold— head stopped up and took some snuff to make him sneeze—a laughable time. *W.M.H.

"TEN ELBO CHAIRS…"

Most of the first settlers who arrived in Chester County during the period from 1680 to 1730 were of English and Welsh origin. They brought with them an affinity for distinctive furniture styles, which they quickly duplicated in their new country. One such furniture form is the wainscot chair.

Wainscot is a term used to describe furniture assembled with mortise and tenon joints to create a framework for supporting panels—in the case of chairs, back and seat panels. The back panels, as evident in the chair opposite, have a strong architectural component to them. The "joyners," or the craftsmen who produced such furniture, while closely allied to house carpenters, specialized in table frames, stools, cabinet doors, heads of beds, and chests of drawers, in addition to chairs.

Wainscot chairs are closely aligned with Chester County, although few have survived with a provenance relating to Chester County families. An exception is the chair illustrated here, which descended in the Bonsall and Hibberd families. Joseph Hibberd was a Quaker joiner who lived and worked in Chester County until his death in 1737. Many wainscot chairs have a shaped, cutout crest rail displaying two curved peaks around a central lunette. This crest rail design is often referred to as a Chester County crest rail, and its shape is unique in American furniture forms.

While the rigid and straight form of wainscot chairs does not appeal to our modern sense of comfort, the chairs were in actuality more comfortable than they appear. An integral part of the wainscot chair would have been a plush pillow, called a squab, which was placed loose on the seat. Squabs were often made from expensive silk or wool imported fabric, a large selection of which was available in Philadelphia even early in the 18th century. When one envisions a highly stuffed pillow on the chair pictured here, the high stance of the arms and proportionality of the chair begin to make sense. Here we have one more glimpse into the level of sophistication that existed in the homes of many early Chester County landowners. "Elbo chairs," listed in an inventory of Joseph Hibbert's estate, are arm chairs, so called as they provide a place to rest one's elbows.

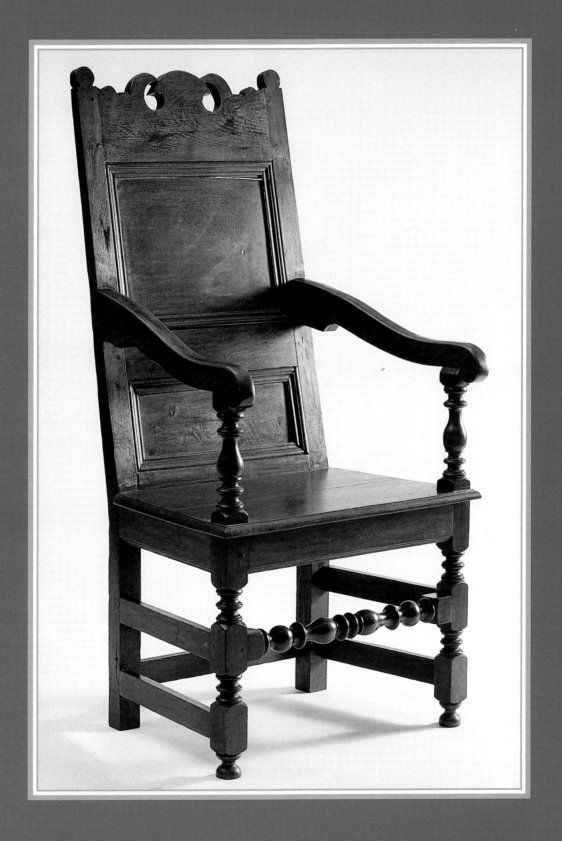

Chester County Day Buffet Dinner

Italian-Style Roasted Peppers and Crostini
(PAGE 23)

Veal Medallions with Apricot Horseradish Sauce
(PAGE 27)

Stuffed Mushrooms
(PAGE 23)

Apple-Spinach Salad
(PAGE 44)

Shrimp with Pernod on Rice
(PAGE 80)

Grilled Pork Tenderloin with Peach Demi-Glace
(PAGE 62)

Brussels Sprouts with Poppy Seeds
(PAGE 89)

New Forest Cider Cake with Whipped Cream
(PAGE 143)

Twinings Lady Grey or Darjeeling Tea

*BRUSSELS SPROUTS WITH POPPY SEEDS

2 pounds large brussels sprouts
2 cups chicken stock or water
2 garlic cloves, finely chopped
2 tablespoons olive oil
Grated zest of 1 lemon
1 tablespoon poppy seeds
Salt and freshly ground pepper to taste
Sugar to taste

Cut the stems from the brussels sprouts and cut into halves lengthwise. Discard any wilted outside leaves. Bring the chicken stock to a boil in a large saucepan. Add the brussels sprouts. Simmer for 5 to 7 minutes or just until bright green and tender-crisp. Drain well. Sauté the garlic in the olive oil in a large skillet for 1 to 2 minutes. Add the brussels sprouts, lemon zest and poppy seeds. Sprinkle with salt, pepper and sugar and toss for about 1 minute or until heated through. The sprouts may be cooked and refrigerated for several days, but be careful not to overcook during reheating. Yield: 8 servings.

Approx Per Serving: Cal 89; Prot 4 g; Carbo 11 g; T Fat 4 g; 39% Calories from Fat;
Chol <1 mg; Fiber 5 g; Sod 200 mg

BLACK WALNUT WATERSTAIN

5 gallon bucket of walnuts (hulls on)
Water to cover
1 pint denatured alcohol

In the fall gather enough black walnuts to fill a 5 gallon bucket (just after walnuts have fallen). Fill bucket with water to cover, add 1 pint denatured alcohol. Cover tightly and rock bucket to mix. Keep covered for 30 to 45 days—rock occasionally. Ready for use after straining into a clean container. Use as you would any stain—works especially well on rough sawn wood (such as new beams) for an aged look.

—*Charles Carey,* grandfather of Miles F. Glidden

*MR. WILLIAM'S CORN PUDDING

1 egg
1 cup milk
$1/2$ teaspoon salt
$1/2$ teaspoon sugar
$1/2$ teaspoon melted butter
Cayenne pepper to taste
1 cup cooked corn

Beat the egg in a medium bowl until frothy. Add the milk, salt, sugar, butter and cayenne pepper and mix well. Stir in the corn. Pour the mixture into a greased $1^1/2$-quart casserole. Bake at 350 degrees for 45 minutes or until set and golden brown. Yield: 4 servings.

Approx Per Serving: Cal 107; Prot 5 g; Carbo 14 g; T Fat 4 g; 34% Calories from Fat;
Chol 63 mg; Fiber 1 g; Sod 348 mg

1/6/1900—There are some places in town where the people do not feel that they can be sociable. It has been charged that some of the churches are rather frigid in their atmosphere, that the clubs are rather exclusive, and the secret societies will not admit just any one who may chance to knock at the door. At market all this is different. The doors swing open for all. The man who has only enough to buy a quarter of a peck of potatoes and get trusted for a quartet of pig's feet is just as welcome as the one who buys sirloin and sweetbreads, and they all may chat together as they go along.

—*Daily Local News*

BAKED CABBAGE

1 medium head cabbage
Salt to taste
1 large sweet onion, sliced
1 tablespoon (about) olive oil
1 (10-ounce) can cream of mushroom soup
1/2 cup shredded Cheddar cheese
Salt and white pepper to taste

Shred the cabbage, rinse and drain. Place in a saucepan with a small amount of lightly salted water. Bring to a boil and reduce the heat. Simmer, covered, until tender, drain well and set aside. Sauté the onion in the desired amount of olive oil in a skillet until tender but not brown. Add the soup and mix well. Add the Cheddar cheese and heat until the cheese melts, stirring constantly. Add salt and pepper and stir in the cabbage. Spoon the cabbage mixture into a greased baking dish. Bake at 350 degrees for 25 minutes. Yield: 6 servings.

Approx Per Serving: Cal 158; Prot 6 g; Carbo 14 g; T Fat 10 g; 52% Calories from Fat;
Chol 10 mg; Fiber 4 g; Sod 438 mg

 10/10/1896—Cranberry sauce! How could we do without it, when cranberries can be had three quarts for 25 cents. Green tomatoes at 20 cents per basket make a health sauce. . . . Chestnuts, walnuts, and shellbarks appeared in abundance. Some new and healthy faces, such as give pleasure to look upon, are in market for the time, time, selling their week's hoard. Chestnuts are plentiful, ripe, but wormy, at 15 cents a quart.

—Morning Republican

COMPANY CARROTS

6 to 8 carrots
2 tablespoons grated onion
2 tablespoons prepared horseradish
$^1/_2$ cup mayonnaise
$^1/_2$ teaspoon salt
$^1/_2$ teaspoon pepper
$^1/_4$ cup dry bread or cracker crumbs
1 tablespoon butter

Slice the carrots as desired. Cook the carrots in a small amount of water in a covered saucepan until tender. Drain, reserving $^1/_4$ cup of the cooking liquid. Place the carrots in a greased 8×8-inch baking dish. Combine the reserved liquid with the onion, horseradish, mayonnaise, salt and pepper in a mixing bowl and mix well. Pour over the carrots, mixing gently. Sprinkle the bread crumbs over the top and dot with the butter. Bake at 375 degrees for 15 minutes. Yield: 6 servings.

Approx Per Serving: Cal 216; Prot 2 g; Carbo 15 g; T Fat 17 g; 70% Calories from Fat;
Chol 19 mg; Fiber 3 g; Sod 402 mg

 8/6/1898—The great quantities of produce coming in by rail and trolley, to say nothing of the home grown stuff, is a sight to gaze upon. Surely all the districts have been heard from and the results sent in.

—*Morning Republican*

CREAMED CELERY

4 cups ($^1/_2$-inch) diagonally sliced celery
2 tablespoons butter
2 tablespoons flour
2 cups milk
1 teaspoon salt
$^3/_4$ cup pecan halves
$^1/_2$ cup dry bread crumbs
2 tablespoons melted butter

Cook the celery in water to cover in a saucepan until tender, drain well and set aside. Melt 2 tablespoons butter in a saucepan. Add the flour and blend well. Stir in the milk gradually. Cook until thickened, stirring constantly. Add the salt and celery and mix well. Pour the mixture into a greased 1$^1/_2$-quart casserole. Sprinkle with the pecans. Toss the bread crumbs with 2 tablespoons melted butter and sprinkle over the pecans. Bake at 400 degrees for 15 minutes. Yield: 6 servings.

Approx Per Serving: Cal 266; Prot 6 g; Carbo 18 g; T Fat 20 g; 66% Calories from Fat;
Chol 32 mg; Fiber 3 g; Sod 653 mg

 3/18/1899—It has been dreamed at times that the nutritive properties of food could be extracted and condensed into pellets or tablets which could be carried about in one's vest pocket and swallowed without interrupting the business or pleasure on hand at the meal hour. As strange things have been done. A beefsteak tablet, another of coffee, a tablet of potatoes, and one or two of apple pie and milk might be handy, but they won't quite take the place of a table with its flashing glass and its social chat.

—*Morning Republican*

MUSHROOM CASSEROLE

3 to 4 pounds fresh mushrooms
3/4 cup water
1/2 cup butter
1 (8-ounce) package stuffing mix
1/4 cup chopped onion (optional)
1/4 cup chopped celery (optional)
3 cups shredded Cheddar cheese
1 1/4 cups half-and-half

Rinse and slice the mushrooms. Cook the mushrooms in a small amount of water in a large saucepan for several minutes, drain well and set aside. Heat 3/4 cup water and 1/2 cup butter in a saucepan until the butter melts. Combine the stuffing mix, onion and celery in a large mixing bowl. Add the butter mixture and mix well; the stuffing mixture will be dry. Alternate layers of the mushrooms, Cheddar cheese and stuffing mixture in a greased 9×13-inch baking dish until all the ingredients are used ending with the stuffing mixture. Dot with additional butter and drizzle the half-and-half over the top. Bake at 350 degrees for 30 minutes. May substitute mozzarella cheese for the Cheddar cheese. Yield: 10 servings.

Approx Per Serving: Cal 390; Prot 18 g; Carbo 26 g; T Fat 25 g; 56% Calories from Fat;
Chol 72 mg; Fiber 3 g; Sod 680 mg

 Chester County was an important junction of the Underground Railroad's Eastern Line. William Still, a freeborn, black Philadelphian, and Quaker abolitionist Thomas Garrett of Wilmington, Delaware, formed a close partnership which enabled approximately 4,000 runaways to find their way to the first station above the Mason-Dixon Line near Kennett in southern Chester County.

POTATO AND LEEK PIE

4 pounds potatoes
4 medium leeks
8 slices bacon
1 teaspoon vegetable oil
$^1/_4$ cup butter
Salt and pepper to taste
2 cups shredded Cheddar cheese
1 cup half-and-half

Peel the potatoes and cut into bite-size pieces. Cook in water to cover in a saucepan until almost tender, drain and set aside. Slice the leeks, rinse under running water to clean well, drain and set aside. Cut the bacon into pieces, cook in the oil in a skillet until crisp and brown, remove and set aside. Add the butter to the skillet and heat until melted. Add the leeks, salt and pepper and mix well. Cook, covered, over medium heat until tender, stirring occasionally. Layer the potatoes, leeks and bacon in a shallow baking dish. Reserve a small amount of the Cheddar cheese for topping. Sprinkle the remaining cheese over the layers. Drizzle the half-and-half over the top. Sprinkle with the reserved cheese. Bake at 350 degrees for 45 minutes. Yield: 10 servings.

Approx Per Serving: Cal 413; Prot 11 g; Carbo 35 g; T Fat 26 g; 56% Calories from Fat;
Chol 57 mg; Fiber 3 g; Sod 335 mg

 10/23/1897—Mush made its first appearance yesterday. The market had a run on the first output and many turned away unsupplied. The grocers in many cases have gone into the manufacturing of it themselves since it has become so popular. Every one eats mush, but all mush is not good mush.

—*Morning Republican*

222

SWISS SCALLOPED POTATOES

8 red potatoes
1 cup shredded Swiss cheese
1/2 cup sliced green onions with tops
1 tablespoon chopped dillweed
2 tablespoons butter
2 tablespoons flour
1 teaspoon salt
1 cup milk
1 cup sour cream
1/4 cup fine dry bread crumbs
1/2 cup shredded Swiss cheese
1/4 cup melted butter

Cook the potatoes in water to cover until tender, drain well, peel and cut into thin slices to yield 6 to 7 cups. Set the potatoes aside. Toss 1 cup Swiss cheese, green onions and dillweed together and set aside. Melt 2 tablespoons butter in a saucepan. Add the flour and salt and blend well. Stir in the milk gradually. Cook until thickened, stirring constantly. Cook for 2 minutes longer, stirring constantly. Remove from the heat and blend in the sour cream. Layer 1/3 of the potato slices in a buttered shallow 3-quart baking dish. Add layers of half the cheese mixture and half the sauce. Repeat the layers with half the remaining potatoes and all the remaining cheese mixture and sauce, ending with a layer of the potatoes. Combine the bread crumbs, 1/2 cup Swiss cheese and 1/4 cup melted butter in a small bowl and toss until well mixed. Sprinkle over the top. Bake at 350 degrees for 30 to 35 minutes or until bubbly. Yield: 12 servings.

Approx Per Serving: Cal 249; Prot 7 g; Carbo 23 g; T Fat 14 g; 51% Calories from Fat; Chol 39 mg; Fiber 2 g; Sod 331 mg

The best cook will fail to furnish us with an acceptable dish if we have no appetite; but with a good appetite, any dish is welcome.

22

96

*SWEDE (RUTABAGA) AND CARROT MASH

2 medium rutabagas
1 pound carrots
$1/4$ cup butter
$1/2$ teaspoon salt
White pepper to taste

Peel and chop the rutabagas and carrots and place in a saucepan. Add salted water to cover and bring to a boil. Reduce the heat and simmer, covered, for 20 to 30 minutes or until tender. Drain well and mash. Add the butter, salt and pepper and mash until smooth. Serve with any meat dish. Yield: 4 servings.

Approx Per Serving: Cal 220; Prot 4 g; Carbo 27 g; T Fat 12 g; 47% Calories from Fat; Chol 31 mg; Fiber 8 g; Sod 486 mg

8/24/1900 This recipe was handed in by a West Chester lady for the benefit of women kind in general and hard-to-please husbands in particular:

- Sharpen all kinds of fish sauce with lemon juice.
- When using vanilla for flavoring add half a teaspoonful of peach extract.
- A dash of black pepper greatly improves vanilla ice cream.
- Put sugar in water used for basting meats of all kinds. It adds a flavor, especially to veal.
- Add a cup of good date vinegar to the water in which you boil fish, especially if it is salt fish.
- Chocolate is greatly improved by adding a teaspoonful of strong coffee just before serving; a teaspoonful of sherry also helps.
- When baking fish place on the top thin slices of salt pork; it bastes the fish and improves the flavor.
- To give an appetizing flavor to a broiled beefsteak rub a cut onion over the hot platter with the butter.
- Three tablespoonfuls freshly made Japan tea, with a pinch of nutmeg, imparts an indescribable flavor to apple pie.
- To improve sweetbreads and give them a fine flavor soak them in mild lemon juice water an hour, and then boil 20 minutes in beef stock.

—*Daily Local News*

*CREAMED SPINACH MADEIRA

2 (10-ounce) packages frozen chopped spinach
$1/4$ cup butter
1 to 2 tablespoons flour or cornstarch
$1/3$ cup madeira
$1/4$ teaspoon white pepper
$2/3$ cup heavy cream
Freshly ground nutmeg to taste

Cook the spinach according to the package directions, drain well and set aside. Melt the butter in a saucepan. Add the flour and blend well. Add the spinach and stir until well mixed. Cook until the spinach mixture bubbles. Add the wine and pepper and cook until the mixture bubbles. Stir in the cream. Cook for 1 to 2 minutes or until the mixture comes to a gentle simmer. Spoon into a serving bowl and top with nutmeg. Yield: 4 servings.

Approx Per Serving: Cal 317; Prot 6 g; Carbo 12 g; T Fat 27 g; 72% Calories from Fat; Chol 85 mg; Fiber 4 g; Sod 239 mg

 1/23/1897—Sauerkraut is new and many people call for it. It costs 5 cents a dipper. You could find it without your glasses. It has characteristics all of its own, but nevertheless, it is only for those who have a leaning that way.

—*Morning Republican*

STUFFED APPLES

Pace One Restaurant

6 apples
3/4 cup chopped red onion
2 tablespoons butter
2 tablespoons plus 1 teaspoon balsamic vinegar
1/3 teaspoon minced garlic
1/4 cup dried cranberries
1/3 cup coarsely chopped pecans

Core the apples and scoop out the centers of the apples to form shells and place in a lightly greased baking dish. Chop enough of the scooped-out centers to yield 4 cups chopped apple. Sauté the chopped apple and onion in the butter in a skillet until tender. Add the vinegar and garlic and toss to mix. Add the cranberries. Place the mixture in a food processor and pulse until chopped; do not purée. Combine the mixture with the pecans and mix well. Spoon into the apple shells. Bake at 375 degrees for 20 minutes or until the apples are tender. Yield: 6 servings.

Approx Per Serving: Cal 191; Prot 1 g; Carbo 29 g; T Fat 9 g; 39% Calories from Fat;
Chol 10 mg; Fiber 5 g; Sod 41 mg

 12/17/1902—George Palmer utilized a windmill mounted on top of his building (on Market Street) to move machinery which operated displays in his window, pumping water and moving trays of figures.

—Daily Local News

AMBER PICKLES

8 or 9 large ripe (yellow) cucumbers
7 cups sugar
2 cups white distilled vinegar
$1/2$ teaspoon oil of cinnamon
$1/2$ teaspoon oil of cloves
2 (4-ounce) jars maraschino cherries

Peel the cucumbers, discard the seeds and cut into 1-inch cubes. Place the cucumber cubes in a large saucepan. Add boiling water to cover and boil just until tender-crisp. Drain well and rinse in cold water until cool and crisp. Place the cucumbers in a crock or bowl. Combine the sugar, vinegar, oil of cinnamon and oil of cloves in a saucepan. Bring to a boil, stirring until the sugar is completely dissolved. Pour over the cucumbers. Let stand for 24 hours. Drain the syrup into a saucepan. Bring to a boil and pour over the cucumbers. Let stand for 24 hours. Drain the syrup into a saucepan. Bring to a boil and add the cucumbers and undrained cherries. Mix well, ladle into hot sterilized jars and seal with 2-piece lids. Let stand until cool and store in the refrigerator. Yield: variable.

Nutritional information for this recipe is not available.

10/30/1906—Of recent growth in West Chester is the sale of hot frankfurters by street vendors. People seem to take to eating "hot sausages and relishes" very readily. This gives a sort of city twang to our street life. We are growing more and more cosmopolitan, as it were.

—*Daily Local News*

GIL'S DILLS

7 to 9 cucumbers
2 garlic cloves, chopped
1 (6-inch) sprig fresh dill
1/4 cup sugar
1/4 cup non-iodized salt
1 cup vinegar
2 quarts water

Cut the cucumbers lengthwise into fourths and pack into a gallon jar. Add the garlic and dill. Combine the sugar, salt, vinegar and water in a saucepan and bring to a boil, stirring until the sugar and salt dissolve completely. Let stand until cool. Pour the vinegar mixture into the jar. Store, covered, in the refrigerator for 7 days before serving. Yield: variable.

Nutritional information for this recipe is not available.

9/4/1897—The preserving season is at fever heat, in some kitchens at blood heat, and even in others, it runs about the boiling point. The good wife has her sleeves rolled up for business and just at the present time she is not in want of material upon which to operate her splendid talent, acquired in her earlier days. The general order of things call for the putting up of catsup, tomato sauce, cucumber sauce, pickled cabbage and the like, prior to the deluge of the market place, first with peaches, then pears and apples in abundance.
—*Morning Republican*

KENTUCKY SPOON BREAD

2 cups milk
3/4 cup white cornmeal
3 tablespoons butter
1 teaspoon salt
2 to 3 tablespoons sugar
3 egg yolks, beaten
3 egg whites, stiffly beaten

Warm the milk in a large saucepan. Stir in the cornmeal gradually. Cook until the mixture is slightly thickened, stirring constantly. Remove from the heat. Add the butter, salt and sugar and mix well. Stir a small amount of the hot mixture into the egg yolks; stir the egg yolks into the hot mixture. Fold in the egg whites gently. Pour the mixture into a greased casserole. Bake at 375 degrees for 35 minutes or until golden brown. This is a soufflé and must be served immediately from the dish in which it is baked. Yield: 6 servings.

Approx Per Serving: Cal 218; Prot 7 g; Carbo 22 g; T Fat 12 g; 47% Calories from Fat;
Chol 133 mg; Fiber 1 g; Sod 522 mg

 On 10/21/1872, it was reported in a local newspaper that Spring Mill, owned and operated by Samuel Fetters, was probably the busiest grist mill throughout Chester County, operating 18 hours a day (every day except Sunday) to meet the demands of his patrons. (Spring Mill is now known as Gunkle Spring Mill, and is located at the intersection of Route 401 and Moores Road in Malvern, Pennsylvania.)

EASY HOLLANDAISE SAUCE

$^1/_2$ cup (1 stick) butter   3 egg yolks
3 tablespoons cream or half-and-half
3 tablespoons tarragon vinegar
Cayenne pepper to taste

Cut the butter into $^1/_2$-inch cubes and freeze for 30 minutes or longer before making the sauce. Whisk the egg yolks in the top of a double boiler. Add the cream, vinegar and cayenne pepper and whisk until well blended. Place the mixture over hot water and cook until the mixture begins to thicken, whisking frequently. Add the butter several pieces at a time, whisking until the butter is melted and well blended after each addition. The sauce will hold over the hot water for 10 to 15 minutes so it must be made at the last minute. If the sauce breaks down, add a teaspoon of ice water and whisk until the sauce is smooth. Yield: 12 (2-tablespoon) servings.

Approx Per Serving: Cal 96; Prot 1 g; Carbo <1 g; T Fat 10 g; 96% Calories from Fat;
Chol 79 mg; Fiber 0 g; Sod 82 mg

SIMPLE MUSHROOM SAUCE

1 (13-ounce) can mushrooms, drained
2 cups nonfat sour cream
$^1/_4$ cup brandy   1 cup half-and-half
4 ounces bleu cheese or Stilton cheese, crumbled
Parsley or dill to taste

Combine the mushrooms, sour cream, brandy, half-and-half and cheese in a saucepan. Heat to serving temperature over low heat, stirring frequently. Add parsley if the sauce is to be served with fowl or dill if the sauce is for salmon or other fish. Sauce can be thickened by blending in 1 tablespoon flour before heating. Yield: 8 ($^1/_4$-cup) servings.

Approx Per Serving: Cal 179; Prot 8 g; Carbo 15 g; T Fat 8 g; 39% Calories from Fat;
Chol 22 mg; Fiber 1 g; Sod 450 mg

"THIS WORK IN HAND MY FRIEND
MAY HAVE..."

Hetty Brinton stitched this line into her sampler in 1799, following a tradition well established in Chester County early in the century. This example is a presentation sampler, as evidenced by the inclusion of the names of her parents, William and Deborah Brinton, followed by the initials, presumably, of their children. Many presentation samplers included similar religious sentiments. A transcript of her verse is:

How Dreadful is The Sinners Fate
Who Sleap To Wake Nomore
Ho looks And Calls Alass To Late
When Deth Have shet Door
Dream not On Joys Unmixed Hie Below
Tha Fragrant Rose on Thay Thorn do grow
This Work in Hand My Friend May Have
When I am Dead And Laid In The Grave
William an Deborah Brinton IB RB IB WB
BB GB SB DB
Hetty Brinton Her Work
Made in Tha 18 year of Her Age An Dom Ano
1799

The initials stitched in black probably indicate a deceased child. Hetty would have presented her sampler to her parents, and they probably would have framed it and hung it in a prominent place in their home. Displaying such fine needlework was a statement about a family's reverence for female education and their level of sophistication and wealth.

There were, in the 18th century, many schools of needlework in nearby Philadelphia, and it was not unusual for some of the county's wealthier farmers to send their daughters there to train. The earliest known school for needlework in Chester County was Mrs. Hollis' School in Goshen Township, which was in existence in 1765. By 1790 the population of the county was rapidly approaching 30,000, and many more needlework schools were established in the next decade to accommodate the growing demand of the prosperous landowners for their daughters' education. One of the most famous schools was Westtown School, from which the earliest sampler is dated 1799.

Hetty Brinton's sampler, worked in a balanced format with delicate design and execution, displays a knowledge of the English sampler tradition. However, the floral border on all four sides, the stylized trees and flowers, and the chickens stitched in the lower row give it a distinctive Chester County milieu. Many such samplers have survived to give witness to the rural, but sophisticated, lives that so many Chester County residents enjoyed in the 18th and 19th centuries.

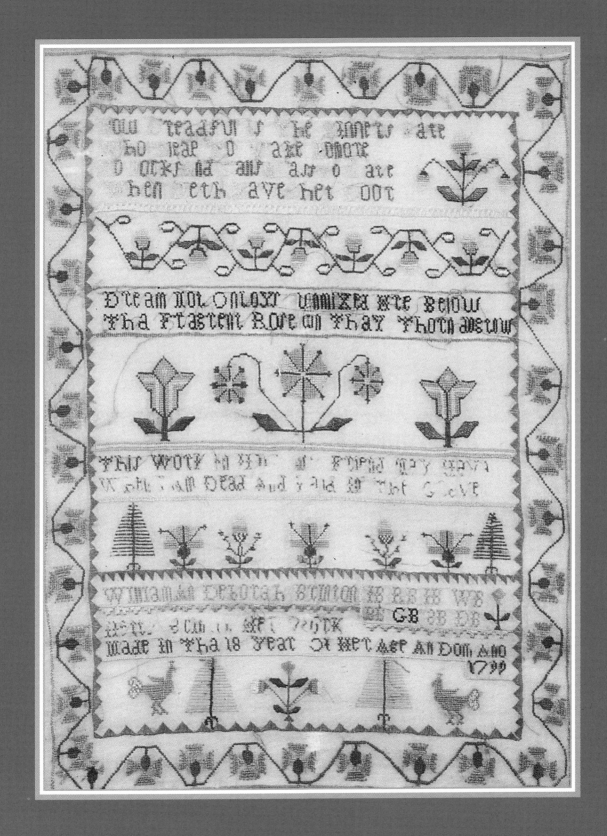

Hunt Brunch

Minted Melon and Grapefruit
(PAGE 45)

Nana's Quick Sticky Buns
(PAGE 117)

Dorothy's Superb Italian Coffee Cake
(PAGE 115)

Cheese Grits
(PAGE 112)

Blueberry French Toast
(PAGE 118)

Make-Ahead Brunch Eggs
(PAGE 109)

Bishop's Downfall
(PAGE 29)

Twinings English Breakfast Tea or Irish Breakfast Tea

ASPARAGUS WITH LEMON CAPER SAUCE

1 pound fresh asparagus spears
1/4 cup water
1 tablespoon vinegar
8 eggs
Lemon Caper Sauce

Snap the tough ends from the asparagus, rinse well and place in a shallow 1-quart microwave-safe dish. Add 1/4 cup water. Microwave, covered, on High for 7 minutes. Drain the asparagus and divide among 4 au gratin dishes. Keep the asparagus warm in a 200-degree oven. Bring 3 inches of water with the vinegar to a boil in a 3-quart saucepan. Break 1 egg into a shallow dish. Stir the boiling water to produce a swirl. Slip the egg into the swirl and cook for 2 to 3 minutes. Remove the egg with a slotted spoon and place on the asparagus. Repeat with the remaining eggs and place 2 poached eggs in each dish. Spoon the Lemon Caper Sauce over the eggs and asparagus and serve immediately. Yield: 4 servings.

LEMON CAPER SAUCE

1/4 cup butter
Juice of 1 lemon
2 tablespoons (heaping) drained capers

Microwave the butter in a 1-cup glass measure until the butter melts. Whisk in the lemon juice and add the capers.

Approx Per Serving: Cal 280; Prot 15 g; Carbo 8 g; T Fat 22 g; 68% Calories from Fat;
Chol 456 mg; Fiber 2 g; Sod 403 mg

CARACAS EGGS

4 ounces dried beef
2 tablespoons butter
2 cups shredded American cheese
1 teaspoon chili powder
2 cups stewed tomatoes
6 eggs
8 thin slices bread
2 tablespoons (about) butter

Shred the dried beef. Melt 2 tablespoons butter in a large heavy skillet. Add the dried beef, American cheese, chili powder and tomatoes. Cook over low heat until the mixture bubbles and the cheese is melted, stirring frequently. Beat the eggs in a bowl. Add to the skillet. Cook until the mixture thickens, stirring frequently. Toast the bread and spread with 2 tablespoons butter. Place 2 slices buttered toast on each of 4 plates. Spoon the egg mixture over the toast. Yield: 4 servings.

Approx Per Serving: Cal 674; Prot 35 g; Carbo 35 g; T Fat 42 g; 57% Calories from Fat; Chol 415 mg; Fiber 1 g; Sod 2510 mg

 How to keep eggs for two years! "2 lbs. coarse salt boiled 10 minutes in 1 gallon rainwater. Pour oft into jar when nearly cool. Stir in 5 tablespoons of quick lime. Let it stand til next day, then put in eggs. Keep tightly covered until wanted."

Sarah Dilworth Woodward (1869–1960)

*MAKE-AHEAD BRUNCH EGGS

1 (20-ounce) loaf French bread
8 ounces sweet bulk sausage
8 ounces hot bulk sausage
1 large onion
12 to 18 eggs
1/2 cup milk
2 cups shredded sharp Cheddar cheese

Cut the bread into 1/2-inch-thick slices and set aside. Cook the sweet and hot sausages with the onion in a skillet until the sausages are brown and crumbly, stirring frequently. Drain well and set aside. Beat the eggs with the milk in a mixing bowl. Cover the bottom of a buttered 9×13-inch baking pan with half the bread slices. Add layers of half the sausage mixture and half the cheese. Repeat the layers with the remaining bread, sausage mixture and cheese. Pour the egg mixture over the layers. Cover the pan with buttered foil and refrigerate for 8 to 12 hours. Bake, covered, with the foil, at 350 degrees for 30 minutes. Bake, uncovered, for 10 minutes longer or until set and golden brown. May add 8 ounces sliced fresh mushrooms to this brunch dish. Yield: 8 servings.

Approx Per Serving: Cal 599; Prot 34 g; Carbo 41 g; T Fat 32 g; 49% Calories from Fat;
Chol 434 mg; Fiber 2 g; Sod 1131 mg

 3/24/1894—The price of eggs yesterday was something remarkable when it is considered that Easter was but a few hours off. Several stores in West Chester were selling them as low as 13 cents a dozen, and in none of them were they higher than 16 cents.
—*Morning Republican*

SPANAKOPITA

1 (10-ounce) package frozen chopped spinach, thawed
3 eggs
6 tablespoons flour
2 cups small curd cottage cheese
2 cups shredded Cheddar cheese
1 teaspoon salt
Pepper to taste

Drain the spinach, squeeze dry and set aside. Beat the eggs in a mixing bowl. Add the flour and beat until smooth. Add the spinach, cottage cheese, Cheddar cheese, salt and pepper and mix well. Pour into a greased 2-quart baking dish. Bake at 350 degrees for 1 hour or until set and golden brown. Let stand for several minutes before serving. Yield: 6 servings.

Approx Per Serving: Cal 302; Prot 23 g; Carbo 11 g; T Fat 18 g; 55% Calories from Fat;
Chol 156 mg; Fiber 2 g; Sod 948 mg

11/18/1899—In no town in this great country of ours can one come nearer getting provender which is fresh, clean, and wholesome than right here in West Chester. The butchers handle their meats with the greatest care, the dairymen and creamery people place at out disposal naught but the production of the richest cream, to which "oleo" is neither kith nor kin. The proprietors of the poultry yards are far above the perpetration of the act of sending anything in the shape of eggs to market which are not pure and sound—except when they make a mistake, and when eggs are 4 cents each—and the turkeys, chicken, ducks and guineas are prepared for the consumer with the greatest care and skill.
—*Morning Republican*

NEW ENGLAND RED FLANNEL HASH

4 pounds potatoes
1 pound carrots
1 medium or large onion
4 (15-ounce) cans beets
2 (12-ounce) cans corned beef
Salt and pepper to taste
$^1/_2$ cup (about) margarine

Peel the potatoes and carrots. Cut the potatoes, carrots and onion into large pieces. Drain the beets. Grind the vegetables and place in a large mixing bowl. Chop the corned beef and add to the bowl with salt and pepper. Mix the ingredients together very well with clean hands. Pat the mixture into 1 large or 2 smaller greased baking pans. Dot with the margarine. Bake at 325 degrees for $2^1/_2$ hours. Yield: 8 servings.

Approx Per Serving: Cal 566; Prot 29 g; Carbo 59 g; T Fat 25 g; 39% Calories from Fat;
Chol 73 mg; Fiber 8 g; Sod 1430 mg

 8/4/1900—The Chicago beef market here is a good one. That is to say, nearly all of the stores selling fresh meat sell that brand almost exclusively and all because their customers appear to like it better than that born, raised and slaughtered on Chester County farms. They say it is more tender. A deal of the Chester County kind admits that it is more tender, but he says that the sole reason for this feature is that the time elapsing between the killing and that of cooking is a couple of weeks or longer—and time, with the help of ice, tones down the tough Texsies, and that's why people are fond of it.

—Daily Local News

*CHEESE GRITS

4 cups water   1 teaspoon salt
1 cup uncooked grits $1/2$ cup butter
1 (6-ounce) roll garlic cheese
2 eggs $2/3$ cup (about) milk

Bring the water with the salt to a boil in a large saucepan. Stir in the grits gradually. Cook until thickened, stirring frequently. Cut the butter and cheese into pieces and add to the grits, stirring until melted and well blended. Remove from the heat. Beat the eggs in a 1-cup measure. Add enough of the milk to measure 1 cup. Stir the egg mixture into the grits. Pour into a greased 2-quart casserole. Bake at 350 degrees for 30 to 40 minutes or until light brown. May substitute Velveeta cheese and garlic to taste for the garlic cheese. Yield: 4 servings.

Approx Per Serving: Cal 547; Prot 16 g; Carbo 36 g; T Fat 38 g; 62% Calories from Fat;
Chol 204 mg; Fiber 1 g; Sod 1430 mg

CHICKEN POT PIE

Cover one stewing hen with water and bring to a boil. Into the pot add a couple of stalks of celery, 2 to 3 carrots, an onion that has been cut up, some peppercorns and salt. Reduce the heat and simmer for about 2 hours. Remove from the burner. When the chicken has cooled, take the meat off the bones and remove the skin. Set aside. Strain the broth, and pour it into the pot again and bring it to a slow rolling boil. Gently drop the pot pie noodles into the liquid, a few at a time, and cook until done (about 2 to 3 minutes) and then add the chicken. Serve in a deep plate or bowl. It will taste even better on the second day and on the third day serve over pancakes.

NOODLES

For the pot pies, mix in a bowl by hand, 2 cups flour, $3/4$ cup milk, 2 teaspoons baking powder, $1/4$ cup shortening, 1 teaspoon salt. Put dough onto a floured board and roll out very, very thin. Cut pastry into 1-inch squares.

—Susy's great Granny Landis

SWISS POTATO KUGEL

1 cup finely chopped onion
2 tablespoons butter
4 cups shredded cooked potatoes
2 cups shredded Swiss cheese
1/4 cup flour
1 teaspoon salt
1/4 teaspoon pepper
3 eggs
3/4 cup half-and-half

Sauté the onion in the butter in a large skillet until tender. Remove from the heat. Add the potatoes and mix well. Toss the cheese with the flour, salt and pepper and add to the skillet, mixing well. Beat the eggs with the half-and-half. Mix into the potato mixture. Spoon the mixture into a greased 9×9-inch baking pan. Bake at 350 degrees for 20 to 30 minutes or until set and golden brown. May refrigerate, covered, for 8 to 12 hours and let stand at room temperature for 30 minutes before baking. May add fresh tomato slices and fresh thyme for variety. Yield: 6 servings.

Approx Per Serving: Cal 364; Prot 17 g; Carbo 30 g; T Fat 20 g; 49% Calories from Fat;
Chol 161 mg; Fiber 2 g; Sod 570 mg

Circa 1862—Miss Anna M. Church advertises that this is leap-year, and she "will wait no longer;" that she is twenty-one years old, healthy, prepossessing, medium size, full chest, educated, prudent, large sparkling eyes, long black flowing hair, and as full of fun as a chestnut full of meat, and born to make some man happy, and wants a home. She concludes by asking, "Does anyone want me?"

BANANA QUICK BREAD

¹/2 cup butter, softened
1 cup sugar
2 eggs
2 cups flour, sifted
1 teaspoon baking soda
¹/2 teaspoon salt
3 very ripe bananas, mashed
¹/3 cup chopped walnuts

Cream the butter and sugar in a mixing bowl until light and fluffy. Add the eggs and beat until well blended. Mix the flour, baking soda and salt together. Add the creamed mixture and beat until well blended. Beat in the bananas. Stir the walnuts into the batter. Pour the batter into a greased 5×9-inch loaf pan. Bake at 350 degrees for 50 minutes or until a cake tester inserted in the center comes out clean. Cool the loaf in the pan for 10 to 15 minutes before turning onto a wire rack to cool completely. This bread is very moist and the flavor is much better the next day.
Yield: 10 servings.

Approx Per Serving: Cal 323; Prot 5 g; Carbo 48 g; T Fat 13 g; 36% Calories from Fat;
Chol 67 mg; Fiber 2 g; Sod 350 mg

11/26/1906—The typical Thanksgiving centerpiece is composed of fruits rather than of flowers, but it is not impossible to find some sort of woodland decoration, if a little effort is made. Laurel can be placed in water, is glossy and pretty, and will remain fresh for weeks.

—*Daily Local News*

*DOROTHY'S SUPERB ITALIAN COFFEE CAKE

2^1/2 cups flour
^{3}/4 cup sugar
1 cup packed brown sugar
1 teaspoon nutmeg
^{1}/2 teaspoon salt
^{3}/4 cup vegetable oil
1 teaspoon baking soda
1 cup buttermilk
1 egg
2 teaspoons cinnamon

Combine the flour, sugar, brown sugar, nutmeg and salt in a large mixing bowl and mix well. Add the oil and mix well. Reserve ^{3}/4 cup of the mixture. Dissolve the baking soda in the buttermilk. Add the buttermilk mixture and the egg to the flour mixture in the mixing bowl and beat until smooth. Pour into a greased and floured 9×13-inch cake pan. Add the cinnamon to the reserved mixture and mix well. Sprinkle over the batter. Bake at 350 degrees for 30 minutes or until golden brown. Yield: 12 servings.

Approx Per Serving: Cal 347; Prot 4 g; Carbo 51 g; T Fat 14 g; 37% Calories from Fat;
Chol 18 mg; Fiber 1 g; Sod 236 mg

12/26/1889—On Christmas Eve, the firm of Charles Huston & Sons, of Coatesville, (Lukens), presented each married man employed in the mills with a fine large turkey; to each single man $1, and each boy 50 cents.

—Daily Local News

DANISH PUFF

1 cup flour
$^1/_2$ cup butter, softened
2 tablespoons water
$^1/_2$ cup butter
1 cup water
1 cup flour
3 eggs
1 teaspoon almond extract
1 recipe confectioners' sugar icing
$^1/_2$ cup slivered almonds

Combine the flour and $^1/_2$ cup softened butter in a mixing bowl and mix until crumbly. Sprinkle with 2 tablespoons water and mix well by hand until mixture forms a dough. Form the dough into two 3×10-inch strips on greased baking sheets. Combine $^1/_2$ cup butter and 1 cup water in a saucepan. Bring to a boil. Add 1 cup flour all at once and mix vigorously until the mixture forms a ball. Remove from the heat. Add the eggs 1 at a time, beating vigorously after each addition until completely blended. Beat in the almond extract. Spread evenly over the strips on the baking sheet. Bake at 350 degrees for 1 hour. Let stand until cool. Spread the icing over the top and sprinkle with almonds. Yield: 8 servings.

Approx Per Serving: Cal 396; Prot 8 g; Carbo 26 g; T Fat 29 g; 67% Calories from Fat;
Chol 142 mg; Fiber 2 g; Sod 260 mg
Nutritional information does not include confectioners' sugar icing.

In 1794, Philadelphia Yearly Meeting, the governing body of Pennsylvania's Quakers, appointed a committee to "establish a school that would provide the children of Friends with a religiously guarded education." Financed by wealthy Friends, Westtown School was founded in 1799 as a coeducational boarding school, exclusively for the children of Friends.

*NANA'S QUICK STICKY BUNS

$^1/_3$ cup packed dark brown sugar
$^1/_4$ cup light corn syrup
$^1/_4$ cup butter
1 teaspoon vanilla extract
$^1/_4$ cup coarsely chopped pecans
1 (8-count) package refrigerator crescent rolls

Place the brown sugar, corn syrup and butter in an 8-inch round cake pan. Place in the oven while preheating to 375 degrees. Remove from the oven when the butter is melted, approximately 10 minutes. Add the vanilla and pecans and stir until well mixed.

Unwrap the crescent roll dough but do not unroll. Cut the dough into 8 slices. Arrange the slices cut side down in the prepared pan. Bake at 375 degrees for 15 minutes or until golden brown.

Cool in the pan on a wire rack for 10 minutes. Invert onto a serving plate. Serve warm.
Yield: 8 servings.

Approx Per Serving: Cal 241; Prot 2 g; Carbo 28 g; T Fat 14 g; 51% Calories from Fat;
Chol 16 mg; Fiber 1 g; Sod 291 mg

Ann Marsh (1717–1797) succeeded her mother Elizabeth as Philadelphia's premier Quaker needlework schoolmistress. When she retired about 1794, she moved to Willistown Township in Chester County to live with her niece. After her death, both her and her mother's possessions, including many important early samplers, were divided among her niece's seven daughters.

*BLUEBERRY FRENCH TOAST

12 slices day-old bread
16 ounces cream cheese
1 cup fresh or frozen blueberries
12 eggs
2 cups milk
1/3 cup maple syrup or honey
Blueberry Sauce

Trim the crusts from the bread and cut the slices into 1-inch cubes. Place half the bread cubes in a greased 9×13-inch baking pan. Cut the cream cheese into 1-inch cubes and arrange over the bread cubes. Add layers of blueberries and the remaining bread. Beat the eggs in a large mixing bowl. Add the milk and maple syrup and beat until well blended. Pour the mixture over the bread. Refrigerate, covered, for 8 to 12 hours. Bake, covered, at 350 degrees for 30 minutes. Bake, uncovered, for 25 minutes longer or until golden brown. Serve with the Blueberry Sauce.
Yield: 6 servings.

BLUEBERRY SAUCE

1 cup sugar
2 tablespoons cornstarch
1 cup water
1 cup fresh or frozen blueberries
1 tablespoon butter

Mix the sugar and cornstarch in a saucepan. Stir in the water gradually. Add the blueberries and butter. Cook over medium heat for 8 to 10 minutes or until thickened, stirring constantly.

Approx Per Serving: Cal 798; Prot 24 g; Carbo 81 g; T Fat 43 g; 48% Calories from Fat; Chol 524 mg; Fiber 2 g; Sod 616 mg

FABULOUS FRENCH TOAST

$1/2$ cup butter
1 cup packed brown sugar
2 tablespoons corn syrup
1 (20-ounce) loaf French bread
5 eggs
$1^1/2$ cups milk
1 teaspoon vanilla extract

Melt the butter in a 9×13-inch baking pan sprayed with nonstick cooking spray. Add the brown sugar and corn syrup and blend well. Spread the mixture evenly in the pan. Cut the bread into $3/4$- to 1-inch slices. Arrange the slices tightly in the prepared pan. Combine the eggs, milk and vanilla in a blender container and process until smooth. Pour the mixture over the bread. Refrigerate, covered, for 8 to 12 hours. Bake, uncovered, at 350 degrees for 30 minutes or until golden brown. Garnish with a sprinkle of confectioners' sugar. Yield: 6 servings.

Approx Per Serving: Cal 651; Prot 16 g; Carbo 93 g; T Fat 24 g; 33% Calories from Fat;
Chol 227 mg; Fiber 3 g; Sod 837 mg

 10/20/1900—This is the opening of the hot cake or waffle season, and it is having its effect in the butter market. The demand is growing and farmers are keeping their top eye open for the proper time to strike for an additional five cents in the value of goods. They'll not wait long, either.

—*Daily Local News*

PUFF PANCAKE

3 eggs
1/2 cup flour
1/2 cup milk
1/2 teaspoon salt
3 tablespoons melted butter
Apple Syrup

Place an 8-inch cast-iron skillet in the freezer for 10 to 15 minutes. Combine the eggs, flour, milk and salt in a blender or food processor and process until well blended; do not beat. Pour the melted butter into the frozen skillet, tilting to cover the bottom of the skillet. Add the batter. Bake in a preheated 450-degree oven for 10 to 15 minutes or until golden brown. Serve with the Apple Syrup. May serve with hot stewed fruit or maple syrup and butter. Yield: 4 servings.

APPLE SYRUP

2 cups packed brown sugar
2 cups apple cider
2 tablespoons butter
1 teaspoon lemon juice
1/2 teaspoon cinnamon
1/2 teaspoon nutmeg

Combine the brown sugar and cider in a saucepan. Heat over medium heat until the brown sugar dissolves, stirring frequently. Add the butter, lemon juice, cinnamon and nutmeg and mix well. Cook until the syrup is slightly thickened, stirring frequently.

Approx Per Serving: Cal 731; Prot 8 g; Carbo 135 g; T Fat 19 g; 23% Calories from Fat;
Chol 202 mg; Fiber 1 g; Sod 546 mg

PUSHOVER POPOVERS

1 cup flour
1 cup milk
4 eggs
Dash of salt
Herbs to taste

Combine the flour, milk and eggs in a mixing bowl and beat with a fork just until blended. Add the salt and herbs. Refrigerate, covered, for 4 hours or up to 12 hours. Fill 8 well-greased custard cups half full with the batter. Arrange the custard cups on a baking sheet. Place in a cold oven. Bake at 450 degrees for 30 minutes. Reduce the temperature to 300 degrees. Bake for 8 minutes longer. Yield: 8 servings.

Approx Per Serving: Cal 113; Prot 6 g; Carbo 14 g; T Fat 4 g; 30% Calories from Fat;
Chol 110 mg; Fiber <1 g; Sod 47 mg

12/20/1888—Christmas trees, principally cedars, are coming from points some distance from Chester County. Prices range from 35 cents to $1, according to size and shape.

12/04/1901—Christmas decorations which trim evergreens are traditional in cities of German descent such as Reading. The tradition is just beginning to take hold in Chester County.

—*Daily Local News*

"...NEW AND FASHIONABLE PLATE, AT THE MOST REASONABLE RATES"

In the early 18th century, wealthy Chester County residents were greatly influenced by the current social and consumer trends in nearby Philadelphia. A sure sign of prestige and wealth was the ownership of plate, or silver. Philadelphia was home to several accomplished silversmiths whose commissioned work was also well known among the county's gentry.

A major influence on the development of specialized forms of silver and on the social customs in both 18th-century Philadelphia and Chester County was the rise in popularity of tea drinking. Tea quickly evolved from a beverage taken plain to one in which cream (or milk) and sugar were added, as well as hot water to regulate its strength. Taking tea became a daily ritual, and specialized forms of silver enhanced the enjoyment of this part of daily life. Besides teapots, silversmiths designed sugar bowls, milk pots (known today as creamers, milk pots were small silver pitchers, often following the form of a larger teapot), salvers (trays to place under pots), hot water jugs, tea caddy spoons, tea strainers, and teaspoons.

Many such specialized items in the collection of CCHS attest to the good taste and wealth of some 18th- and 19th-century county residents. Pictured here, in addition to a punch strainer and salt spoons, is a tea caddy spoon made by Joseph Lownes, who worked in Philadelphia from 1780 to 1816. This is an item that is a highly specialized form, which would have been added to a family's inventory of fine silver only after first the teapot and then a sugar bowl and/or milk pot had been purchased. Items in a service did not necessarily have to match each other, and silver pieces joined porcelain or earthenware pieces on the tea table.

A form of silver that we take for granted today also had its origin on the tea table. The teaspoon, aptly named for its function, was a spoon designed to fit the smaller handleless teacups from which 18th-century Americans drank their tea. Prior to this time, spoons were one large, multi-purpose size. With the emergence of the teaspoon came other specialized spoons, such as salt spoons, sugar spoons, mustard spoons, and serving spoons. This same refinement in dining, innovative in the 18th and 19th centuries, adds much to our enjoyment of dining and entertaining today.

John Leacock advertised in the *Pennsylvania Gazette* on July 27, 1751, for his "... new and fashionable plate ..."

Afternoon Tea Party

Scones Windsor Court Hotel
(PAGE 133)

Lemon Curd
(PAGE 139)

Strawberry Jam

Clotted Cream

Cucumber Sandwiches
(PAGE 127)

Egg and Cress Sandwiches
(PAGE 127)

Chicken and Walnut Salad Sandwiches
(PAGE 126)

Cheesy Tea Sandwiches
(PAGE 126)

Shortbread Hearts
(PAGE 138)

Amaretto Apricot Cookies
(PAGE 136)

Mini-Jammy Buns
(PAGE 129)

Highland Farm Brownies
(PAGE 137)

Twinings Prince of Wales Tea or Green Tea and Mint

CHESTER COUNTY HOSPITALITY TEA

3 quarts water
4 tea bags
Sugar to taste
3 cups orange juice
1 tablespoon (heaping) whole cloves

Bring the water to a boil in a large saucepan. Add the tea bags and steep for 4 minutes. Discard the tea bags. Add the desired amount of sugar, orange juice and cloves and stir until the sugar dissolves. Let stand for 5 minutes. Strain the tea mixture into a pitcher and discard the cloves. Serve cold over ice or reheat to serve hot. Yield: 12 servings.

Nutritional information for this recipe is not available.

*CRANBERRY TEA

4 cups water
4 cups cranberry juice cocktail
2 tea bags
2 cinnamon sticks
10 whole cloves
Juice of $1/2$ lemon
$1/2$ cup sugar

Combine the water, cranberry juice, tea bags, cinnamon sticks and cloves in a large saucepan. Bring to a simmer and simmer for 5 to 10 minutes. Remove the tea bags and add the lemon juice and sugar, stirring until the sugar dissolves. Keep hot, removing the cinnamon sticks and cloves if the tea is to be held for 30 minutes or longer. Yield: 8 servings.

Approx Per Serving: Cal 121; Prot <1 g; Carbo 31 g; T Fat <1 g; 1% Calories from Fat;
Chol 0 mg; Fiber <1 g; Sod 3 mg

*CHEESY TEA SANDWICH SPREAD

8 ounces cream cheese, softened
2 cups shredded Cheddar cheese
$^1/_3$ cup Major Grey's chutney   2 teaspoons prepared mustard
2 tablespoons minced chives
$^1/_2$ cup chopped walnuts

Combine the cream cheese, Cheddar cheese, chutney, mustard, chives and walnuts in a mixing bowl and mix well. To serve, spread thin slices of multigrain bread with softened butter. Spread the desired amount of the cheese mixture on half the slices, top with the remaining slices and cut each sandwich diagonally into triangles. Yield: 3$^1/_3$ cups.

Approx Per Recipe: Cal 2417; Prot 83 g; Carbo 95 g; T Fat 192 g; 71% Calories from Fat;
Chol 487 mg; Fiber 3 g; Sod 3117 mg
Nutritional information is for the entire amount of the recipe and
does not include the multigrain bread or the softened butter.

*CHICKEN AND WALNUT SALAD SANDWICHES

4 boneless skinless chicken breasts
$^1/_4$ cup chopped walnuts
$^1/_4$ teaspoon minced fresh thyme
$^1/_8$ teaspoon minced garlic
$^1/_2$ cup mayonnaise   Salt and pepper to taste
30 slices bread

Cook the chicken as desired, cool and cut into chunks. Place the chicken in a food processor fitted with a metal blade and process until finely chopped. Add the walnuts, thyme, garlic, mayonnaise and salt and pepper and process until smooth. Cut the crusts from the bread. Spread the chicken mixture over half the bread slices. Top with the remaining slices. Cut the sandwiches diagonally into triangles. Yield: 30 sandwiches.

Approx Per Sandwich: Cal 162; Prot 10 g; Carbo 17 g; T Fat 6 g; 32% Calories from Fat;
Chol 23 mg; Fiber 1 g; Sod 200 mg

*CUCUMBER SANDWICHES

3 ounces cream cheese, softened
1 tablespoon mayonnaise
1 teaspoon minced fresh dill, or $^1/_4$ teaspoon dried dill
$^1/_4$ teaspoon Worcestershire sauce
1 small cucumber
6 very thin slices rye bread

Mix the cream cheese, mayonnaise, dill and Worcestershire sauce in a small bowl. Score the unpeeled cucumber lengthwise with a fork and cut crosswise into very thin slices. Cut four $1^3/_4$-inch rounds from each bread slice with a biscuit cutter. Reserve the trimmings for another purpose. Spread each bread round with a small amount of the cream cheese mixture and top with 2 cucumber slices. Place the open-face sandwiches on damp paper towels on a tray and cover with additional damp paper towels to prevent drying. Refrigerate until serving time.
Yield: 24 sandwiches.

Approx Per Sandwich: Cal 39; Prot 1 g; Carbo 4 g; T Fat 2 g; 46% Calories from Fat;
Chol 4 mg; Fiber 1 g; Sod 67 mg

*EGG AND CRESS SANDWICHES

2 hard-boiled eggs, peeled
1 teaspoon mayonnaise
Watercress to taste   Salt and pepper to taste
Softened butter   Thinly sliced bread

Place eggs in a food processor and pulse to chop coarsely. Add the mayonnaise, watercress and salt and pepper and process until well mixed but still textured. Spread the desired amount of softened butter on the desired number of bread slices. Spread the egg mixture over the top and cover with additional slices, press lightly, trim crusts and cut each into thirds lengthwise.
Yield: 1 recipe egg mixture.

Approx Per Recipe: Cal 188; Prot 13 g; Carbo 1 g; T Fat 14 g; 70% Calories from Fat;
Chol 427 mg; Fiber 0 g; Sod 149 mg
Nutritional information does not include the buttered bread.

*CHEESE BISCUITS

1 cup flour
1/4 teaspoon salt
1 cup shredded sharp Cheddar cheese
1/2 cup butter
1/4 cup (about) orange marmalade

Combine the flour, salt, Cheddar cheese and butter in a bowl and knead until the mixture forms a dough. Shape the dough into walnut-size balls and place each in an ungreased muffin cup. Make a small indentation in the center of each ball. Place a small amount of marmalade in the indentation. Bake at 350 degrees for 20 minutes or until golden brown. May substitute an anchovy, half an olive and/or capers for the marmalade. Yield: 20 biscuits.

Approx Per Biscuit: Cal 96; Prot 2 g; Carbo 8 g; T Fat 7 g; 60% Calories from Fat;
Chol 18 mg; Fiber <1 g; Sod 113 mg

Did you know that the Slinky™ was invented in Chester County. In 1942, Richard James, an engineer from Bryn Mawr noticed that some springs he was working with could "walk." This simple observation made James a millionaire by the time he was 30!

To meet worldwide demand for the Slinky™ Toy, he founded James Industries, Inc., first located in Paoli, Pennsylvania. Several of these "magic springs" reside in the CCHS collection.

*MINI-JAMMY BUNS

Special Teas Tea Room

1 3/4 cups flour
1 tablespoon baking powder
1/4 teaspoon salt
1/4 cup margarine, softened
1/2 cup sugar
1 egg
3 to 4 tablespoons milk
2 to 3 teaspoons black currant jam

Combine the flour, baking powder and salt in a mixing bowl. Add the margarine and cut in until crumbly. Add the sugar and mix well. Beat the egg with the milk. Add to the flour mixture and mix until the mixture forms a stiff dough. Divide the dough into 24 portions and shape each into a smooth ball. Arrange on a lightly greased or parchment paper-lined baking sheet. Make an indentation in each with the handle of a wooden spoon. Fill each hole with 1/8 teaspoonful jam. Sprinkle lightly with additional sugar. Bake at 400 degrees for 10 minutes. Remove to a wire rack to cool slightly. Serve warm. Substitute any favorite jam for black currant and/or add 1/8 teaspoon ground spice of choice to the dough. Yield: 24 buns.

Approx Per Bun: Cal 73; Prot 1 g; Carbo 13 g; T Fat 2 g; 26% Calories from Fat;
Chol 9 mg; Fiber <1 g; Sod 112 mg

 Brigadier General Anthony Wayne, a native of Chester Country, has been called "the best fighting general in American history." His birthplace, Waynesborough, still stands in Easttown Township.

BORROWDALE TEA BREAD

Special Teas Tea Room

1^1/4 cups hot brewed strong black tea
12 ounces raisins or currants
1 cup packed brown sugar
1 egg
2 cups flour
1 tablespoon baking powder
^{1}/2 teaspoon salt

Strain the hot tea if loose tea has been used. Combine the hot tea and the raisins in a bowl. Let stand, covered, for 8 to 12 hours. Grease a 5×9-inch loaf pan and line the bottom with parchment paper or waxed paper. Combine the brown sugar and egg in a mixing bowl and beat until light and fluffy. Mix the flour, baking powder and salt together. Stir into the egg mixture. Add the raisins with any liquid and mix well. Pour into the prepared loaf pan. Bake at 325 degrees for 1^1/2 hours or until a skewer inserted in the center comes out clean. Cool the loaf in the pan on a wire rack. Yield: 12 servings.

Approx Per Serving: Cal 237; Prot 4 g; Carbo 57 g; T Fat 1 g; 3% Calories from Fat;
Chol 18 mg; Fiber 2 g; Sod 236 mg

 In the 1840s there existed in part of North Coventry Township, around Shenkel Church, a strange religious cult called the "Battle Axes of the Lord." Their leaders were Theophilus Gates and Hannah Williamson. They believed in holding all things in common, including sexual favors. Hannah apparently enticed new converts. They promoted "onanism," what today we would call birth control, and nudity, as well as disregarding the Sabbath laws. In 1844, a number of Battle Axes were arrested and convicted of adultery or fornication. The cult continued, however, and after the death of Gates, continued under Hannah's leadership. She evolved a ritual which included skinny dipping in a local pond. However the cult died after the first generation. By 1850 Hannah had left and headed west. Although the Battle Axes have faded into obscurity, the area is still known as Free Love Valley.

—*Anne Wiegle*

CRANBERRY BREAD

2 cups sifted flour
1 cup sugar
1^1/2 teaspoons baking powder
1 teaspoon salt
^{1}/2 teaspoon baking soda
Grated zest and juice of 1 orange
2 tablespoons melted shortening
1 egg, beaten
^{1}/2 cup chopped pecans
2 cups thinly sliced fresh cranberries

Sift the flour, sugar, baking powder, salt and baking soda into a mixing bowl. Combine the orange zest, orange juice and melted shortening in a 1-cup measure. Add enough water to measure ^{3}/4 cup. Stir in the egg. Add the egg mixture to the dry ingredients and mix just until moistened. Fold in the pecans and the cranberries. Spoon into greased 3×7-inch loaf pan. Bake at 350 degrees for 1 hour or until the loaf tests done. Cool on a wire rack, wrap tightly and store for 24 hours before slicing. Yield: 10 servings.

Approx Per Serving: Cal 255; Prot 4 g; Carbo 45 g; T Fat 7 g; 26% Calories from Fat;
Chol 21 mg; Fiber 3 g; Sod 376 mg

The necessity of taking a spring medicine to remove the impurities which have accumulated in the blood during the winter months, and to overcome the long train of debilitating conditions resulting from their retention in the life current, should be apparent to everyone.

PUMPKIN CHOCOLATE CHIP MUFFINS

4 eggs
2 cups sugar
1 (16-ounce) can pumpkin
1^1/2 cups vegetable oil
3 cups flour
2 teaspoons baking soda
2 teaspoons baking powder
1 teaspoon salt
1 teaspoon cinnamon
2 cups miniature chocolate chips
^{1}/2 cup sliced toasted almonds (optional)

Combine the eggs, sugar, pumpkin and oil in a mixing bowl and beat until smooth. Sift the flour, baking soda, baking powder, salt and cinnamon together. Add to the pumpkin mixture and mix well. Stir in the chocolate chips and almonds. Fill greased or paper-lined muffin cups ^{3}/4 full. Bake at 400 degrees for 16 to 20 minutes or until golden brown. May omit the almonds if desired. Yield: 24 muffins.

Approx Per Muffin: Cal 380; Prot 5 g; Carbo 44 g; T Fat 21 g; 49% Calories from Fat;
Chol 35 mg; Fiber 3 g; Sod 254 mg

1/1/1902—The New Year Assembly at the Armory was one of the most brilliant events. Two hundred guests in full dress made a perfect picture, dancing to the two-step and waltz. Handsome decorations in green and red were arranged about the walks; banks of palms filled the windows with festoons of laurel and holly.

—*Daily Local News*

*SCONES WINDSOR COURT HOTEL

2^1/2 cups flour
5 teaspoons baking powder
4 teaspoons sugar
^{1}/8 teaspoon salt
6 tablespoons cold butter
^{3}/4 cup heavy cream
2 eggs, lightly beaten
^{1}/3 cup dried currants (optional)
1 egg
^{1}/3 cup milk
1 tablespoon sugar

Sift the flour, baking powder, 4 teaspoons sugar and salt into a mixing bowl. Cut the butter into small pieces. Add to the flour mixture and cut in the butter until crumbly. Add the cream, the 2 lightly beaten eggs and currants and mix just until the mixture makes a dough.

Pat the dough 1 inch thick on a lightly floured surface and cut with a 2-inch cutter. Arrange the scones on a buttered baking sheet. Beat 1 egg with the milk to make an egg wash. Brush the scones with the egg wash and sprinkle lightly with 1 tablespoon sugar.

Bake at 450 degrees for 13 to 15 minutes or until light golden brown. Yield: 15 scones.

Approx Per Scone: Cal 193; Prot 4 g; Carbo 21 g; T Fat 10 g; 48% Calories from Fat;
Chol 72 mg; Fiber 1 g; Sod 249 mg

GRANDMOTHER'S LEMON CAKE

$^3/4$ cup shortening
$1^1/2$ cups sugar
3 eggs
$2^1/4$ cups flour
$^1/4$ teaspoon salt
$^1/4$ teaspoon baking soda
$^3/4$ cup buttermilk
Grated zest of 1 lemon
$^3/4$ cup chopped nuts (optional)
$^3/4$ cup sugar
Juice of 1 lemon

Cream the shortening and $1^1/2$ cups sugar in a mixing bowl until light and fluffy. Add the eggs and beat until well blended. Mix the flour, salt and baking soda together. Add to the creamed mixture alternately with the buttermilk, mixing well after each addition. Stir in the lemon zest and nuts. Divide the batter among 3 greased 5×9-inch loaf pans.

Bake at 350 degrees for 30 to 35 minutes or until the loaves test done. Blend $^3/4$ cup sugar with the lemon juice and spoon over the warm loaves. May bake the cake in a 9×13-inch cake pan for about 45 minutes. Yield: 30 servings.

Approx Per Serving: Cal 148; Prot 2 g; Carbo 23 g; T Fat 6 g; 35% Calories from Fat;
Chol 21 mg; Fiber <1 g; Sod 43 mg

NUT CAKE

2 cups sugar
1 cup butter, softened
3 eggs
3 cups flour
2 teaspoons baking powder
1/8 teaspoon salt
1 cup milk
2 cups chopped black walnuts

Cream the sugar and butter in a mixing bowl until light and fluffy. Add the eggs 1 at a time, beating well after each addition. Mix the flour, baking powder and salt together. Add to the creamed mixture alternately with the milk, beating well after each addition. Stir in the black walnuts. Pour the batter into 2 greased and floured 5×9-inch loaf pans or five 3×5 1/2-inch loaf pans. Bake at 350 degrees for 1 hour or until the loaves test done. Yield: 20 servings.

Approx Per Serving: Cal 322; Prot 6 g; Carbo 37 g; T Fat 18 g; 7% Calories from Fat; Chol 48 mg; Fiber 1 g; Sod 173 mg

 COUGH SYRUP. "One large handful of hops put into one quart of cold water. Boil down to one pint. Strain. Add one lb. Brown sugar. Boil to a tolerably thick syrup. When cool, add one gill of best brandy or whiskey and bottle."
—*Hannah Mattson Woodward* (1816–1894)

*AMARETTO APRICOT COOKIES

$^1/_2$ cup sugar
$^3/_4$ cup packed brown sugar
1 cup margaraine, softened
1 egg
1 tablespoon amaretto
1 cup flour
1 teaspoon baking soda
$2^1/_2$ cups rolled oats
1 cup finely chopped dried apricots
$^1/_2$ cup chopped almonds

Cream the sugar, brown sugar and margarine in a mixing bowl until light and fluffy. Add the egg and amaretto and beat until blended. Mix the flour and baking soda together. Add to the creamed mixture and mix well. Stir in the oats, apricots and almonds. Drop by teaspoonfuls onto a greased cookie sheet. Bake at 375 degrees for 5 to 10 minutes. Cool on the cookie sheet for 1 to 2 minutes and remove to a wire rack to cool completely. Yield: 60 cookies.

Approx Per Cookie: Cal 78; Prot 1 g; Carbo 10 g; T Fat 4 g; 44% Calories from Fat;
Chol 4 mg; Fiber 1 g; Sod 59 mg

 12/28/1896—Herbert Worth—"I think that more Christmas trees were sold in West Chester this year than ever before. I would estimate that no less than 200 trees were sold here the few days previous to Christmas."

—*Morning Republican*

*HIGHLAND FARM BROWNIES

1/2 cup melted butter
2 (1-ounce) squares unsweetened baking chocolate, melted
2 eggs
1/2 teaspoon vanilla extract
1 cup sugar
1/2 cup flour
1/2 teaspoon salt
1 cup chocolate chips (optional)
1/2 cup chopped pecans (optional)

Blend the melted butter and melted chocolate together in a mixing bowl. Add the eggs and vanilla and mix well. Mix the sugar, flour and salt together. Add to the chocolate mixture and stir until well mixed; do not beat. Stir in the chocolate chips and pecans. Pour the batter into a lightly greased 8×8-inch baking pan. Bake at 375 degrees for 25 to 30 minutes or until brownies pull from the side of the pan. Yield: 12 servings.

Approx Per Serving: Cal 288; Prot 3 g; Carbo 32 g; T Fat 19 g; 55% Calories from Fat;
Chol 56 mg; Fiber 2 g; Sod 188 mg

12/27/1894—A stage coach which was used in the West years ago is to be a feature of the New Year's Eve parade. A band of Indians will attack it many times during the evening. It is to be defended by a party of brave cowboys from the West Ward.

—*Daily Local News*

*SHORTBREAD HEARTS

1$^{1}/_{2}$ cups unsalted butter, softened
1 cup confectioners' sugar
1 teaspoon vanilla extract
3 cups flour
$^{1}/_{2}$ teaspoon salt
$^{1}/_{4}$ cup sugar

Cream the butter and confectioners' sugar in a bowl until light and fluffy. Beat in the vanilla. Sift the flour and salt together. Add to the creamed mixture and mix well. Shape the dough into a log about 3 inches in diameter. Chill in the freezer for about 30 minutes. Cut a V-shaped wedge from the top of the log and gently mold the bottom of the log into a point. Cut the log into $^{1}/_{4}$-inch slices and arrange cut side down on a baking sheet. Sprinkle lightly with the sugar.

Bake at 325 degrees for 15 to 20 minutes or just until until light golden; do not brown. May shape the dough into a ball and roll on a surface lightly sprinkled with additional confectioners' sugar to $^{5}/_{8}$-inch thickness and cut with a 3-inch heart-shaped cookie cutter. Arrange on a baking sheet and chill for 45 minutes. Sprinkle with sugar and bake as above. Yield: 20 cookies.

Approx Per Cookie: Cal 234; Prot 2 g; Carbo 20 g; T Fat 16 g; 62% Calories from Fat;
Chol 44 mg; Fiber 1 g; Sod 84 mg

LEMON CURD TARTLETS

Lemon Curd
48 (1³/4-inch) miniature baked tart shells

Spoon the Lemon Curd into the tart shells and serve immediately. Yield: 48 tartlets.

*LEMON CURD

¹/2 cup lemon juice
Grated zest of 1 lemon
2 cups sugar
1 cup butter
4 eggs, well beaten

Combine the lemon juice and zest with the sugar in a double boiler and mix well. Add the butter and place over boiling water. Heat until the butter melts, stirring constantly. Stir a small amount of the hot mixture into the beaten eggs; stir the eggs into the hot mixture. Cook for 15 minutes or until the mixture mounds slightly when dropped from a spoon, stirring constantly. Chill in the refrigerator.

Approx Per Tartlet: Cal 173; Prot 3 g; Carbo 18 g; T Fat 11 g; 56% Calories from Fat;
Chol 28 mg; Fiber 2 g; Sod 109 mg

"TOGETHER WITH MY SPICE BOX . . ."

Among the many contributions that Chester County artisans have made to the existing body of American decorative arts, three forms are outstanding. The spice box, the fancy redware flowerpot, and the Quaker friendship quilt all display notable and unique characteristics that make them highly prized today among collectors and scholars of Americana.

The spice box had its origin in its English counterpart, which was a form of furniture used only through the early part of the 18th century. In Pennsylvania, however, spice boxes were made throughout the 18th century and came into their most refined and exuberant form in Chester County. Spice boxes are diminutive forms of case furniture; they were used not only for the storage of valuable spices such as nutmeg and ginger, but also for the storage of small personal items, silver and gold buttons, scissors, silver spoons, and other things of value. They were prized pieces of furniture and would have been found in the formal parlor among a family's best furnishings. The elaborate inlay, particularly the line and berry inlay found on many spice boxes, is almost exclusively Chester County.

While the spice box is predominantly 18th-century form, some artisans in 19th-century Chester County were making a different kind of product. Although redware is generally associated with the Pennsylvania German tradition, Quakers in Chester County were also producing pottery made out of the iron-bearing red clay, deposits of which are found throughout Chester County. The most distinctive form of Chester County redware is the fancy flowerpot. The best extant examples exhibit applied ruffles on the upper rim and, also, often on the saucer. A name and date are incised on the body of the pot, often accompanied by other decoration. Although fancy flowerpots, usually commissioned for a special occasion, represent only a small percentage of the business that local potteries were doing, they exhibit an artistry that is distinctively Chester County.

Another tradition in Chester County is that of the Quaker friendship quilt. After about 1825, Quaker friendship quilts were usually made of calicoes, often in a red and green palette and generally in one of the simpler patchwork designs, as opposed to appliqued designs. Names were written or stamped in indelible ink in the center of blocks. Such quilts were group projects, usually made in celebration of an engagement or wedding or as a display of familial love and loyalty. They express Quaker values in their orderliness and sentiment but also exhibit a social liveliness, demonstrating the vitality of Chester County's historical past.

"Together with my Spice Box . . ." is from instructions for the disbursement of her belongings, from the will of Martha Waite of Philadelphia in 1720.

Old-Fashioned Christmas Dinner

Radish Spread with Crackers
(PAGE 21)

Australian Cheese Ball
(PAGE 16)

Apple Squash Bisque
(PAGE 37)

Mixed Greens with Honey Mustard Dressing
(PAGE 51)

Mother's Bohempen Duck
(PAGE 67)

Mr. William's Corn Pudding
(PAGE 90)

Creamed Spinach Madeira
(PAGE 98)

Gingerbread Pudding
(PAGE 184)

Assorted Cookies and Ice Cream

Twinings Earl Grey or Lapsang Souchon Tea

*NEW FOREST CIDER CAKE

²/₃ cup dry or hard cider
1 cup golden raisins
¹/₂ cup butter, softened
¹/₂ cup packed brown sugar
2 eggs
2 cups self-rising flour

Combine the cider and raisins in a bowl. Let the raisins soak overnight. Cream the butter and brown sugar in a mixing bowl until light and fluffy. Add the eggs 1 at a time, beating well after each addition. Add half the flour and mix well.

Add the raisins and cider mixture and mix well. Fold in the remaining flour. Pour into a greased 8×8-inch cake pan. Bake at 350 degrees for 1 hour or until the cake tests done. Yield: 16 servings.

Approx Per Serving: Cal 174; Prot 3 g; Carbo 27 g; T Fat 7 g; 33% Calories from Fat;
Chol 42 mg; Fiber 1 g; Sod 269 mg

 9/15/1900—Cider mills are busy. The output of pure cider vinegar this year ought to be immense, and yet it is safe to say that barrels of the bogus kind will be brought to town and sold before the robins nest again. Bogus vinegar ought to be tabooed more than it is. We rightfully make a big kick against fictitious butter, but the bogus vinegar finds a ready sale at big prices, without anything being said against it. Verily we are queer people along certain lines.

—*Daily Local News*

CHOCOLATE VIENNA CAKE

6 egg yolks   1/2 cup sugar
3/4 cup sifted flour
1 teaspoon baking powder
1 teaspoon salt   6 egg whites
1/2 teaspoon cream of tartar
1/2 cup sugar
1 cup grated unsweetened chocolate
Sweetened Whipped Cream

Beat the egg yolks in a large mixing bowl until thick and lemon-colored. Beat in 1/2 cup sugar gradually. Sift the flour, baking powder and salt together. Add to the egg yolk mixture and beat until well blended. Beat the egg whites with cream of tartar in a mixing bowl until stiff peaks form. Add 1/2 cup sugar gradually, beating until very stiff glossy peaks form. Fold the stiffly beaten egg whites into the egg yolk mixture gently. Fold in the grated chocolate gently. Pour the batter into two 9-inch layer cake pans lined with greased parchment paper. Bake at 350 degrees for 20 minutes or until the cakes spring back when lightly touched. Loosen the cake layers from the sides of the pans and turn onto wire racks to cool completely. Spread the Sweetened Whipped Cream between the layers and over the top and side of the cake. Garnish with flakes of chocolate. Yield: 16 servings.

SWEETENED WHIPPED CREAM

1 teaspoon unflavored gelatin
2 tablespoons cream or milk
2 cups whipping cream, chilled
1/2 cup sifted confectioners' sugar
1 1/2 teaspoons vanilla extract or other flavoring

Soften the unflavored gelatin in the cream in a small bowl. Heat over hot water until the gelatin dissolves completely and set aside. Whip the whipping cream in a mixing bowl until soft peaks form. Add the confectioners' sugar gradually, beating constantly. Add the gelatin mixture and vanilla and whip until stiff peaks form.

Approx Per Serving: Cal 260; Prot 5 g; Carbo 23 g; T Fat 18 g; 59% Calories from Fat;
Chol 122 mg; Fiber 1 g; Sod 213 mg

GRANDMOTHER TOWNSEND-IVISIONS FRUITCAKE

2 pounds seedless raisins   1 pound currants
1 pound candied cherries
1 pound citron   1 cup candied lemon peel
1 cup candied orange peel
4 cups flour   4 teaspoons allspice
4 teaspoons cinnamon
1 teaspoon nutmeg   1 1/2 teaspoons mace
1 pound butter, softened
1 pound brown sugar   12 eggs
2 cups strawberry jam
1 cup molasses   1 cup grape juice
1/4 teaspoon baking soda
1 tablespoon hot water
Brandy

Cut all of the fruit into desired size pieces. Combine the raisins, currants, candied cherries, citron, and lemon and orange peel into a large bowl. Add 1/4 cup of the flour and toss lightly coat the fruit and set aside. Sift the remaining 3 1/2 cups flour, allspice, cinnamon, nutmeg and mace together. Cream the butter and brown sugar together in a very large mixing bowl. Add the eggs 1 at a time, beating well after each addition. Add the jam, molasses and grape juice and mix well. Add the flour mixture and mix until smooth. Fold in the fruit mixture. Spoon into 4 greased and floured 5×9-inch loaf pans.

Bake at 275 degrees for 3 to 4 hours or until firm. Turn the hot loaves onto wire racks. Pour brandy over the hot loaves. Let stand until completely cool. Wrap in foil and store for 2 weeks. Open the foil carefully and pour additional brandy over the loaves. Rewrap tightly. Yield: 100 slices.

Approx Per Slice: Cal 177; Prot 2 g; Carbo 34 g; T Fat 4 g; 22% Calories from Fat;
Chol 35 mg; Fiber 1 g; Sod 69 mg
Nutritional information does not include the brandy.

PEANUT BUTTER TANDY CAKE

2 cups sugar
2 tablespoons butter, softened
4 eggs
1 teaspoon vanilla extract
2 cups flour
1 teaspoon baking powder
$^1/_8$ teaspoon salt
1 cup milk
8 ounces peanut butter
7 ounces milk chocolate

Combine the sugar, butter, eggs and vanilla in a mixing bowl and beat until well blended. Mix the flour, baking powder and salt together. Add to the egg mixture alternately with the milk, beating well after each addition. Pour into a greased and floured 10×15-inch baking pan.

Bake at 350 degrees for 10 to 20 minutes or until golden brown. Spread the peanut butter over the top of the hot cake. Chill, covered, until the peanut butter firms.

Break half the chocolate into pieces and place in a small microwave-safe bowl. Microwave on Medium for 2 minutes or until melted. Spread over half the cake. Repeat with the remaining chocolate. Chill, covered, in the refrigerator. Let stand at room temperature for 30 minutes before cutting into squares. Yield: 24 servings.

Approx Per Serving: Cal 228; Prot 5 g; Carbo 32 g; T Fat 10 g; 37% Calories from Fat;
Chol 41 mg; Fiber 1 g; Sod 109 mg

PINEAPPLE CAKE

2 cups flour
2 cups sugar
2 teaspoons baking soda
$1/2$ teaspoon salt
2 eggs
1 (20-ounce) can crushed pineapple
Cream Cheese Frosting
$1/2$ cup chopped pecans

Combine the flour, sugar, baking soda and salt in a large bowl. Add the eggs and undrained pineapple and stir until well mixed. Pour into a greased and floured 9×13-inch cake pan. Bake at 325 to 350 degrees for 30 to 35 minutes or until the cake tests done. Spread the Cream Cheese Frosting over the warm cake. Sprinkle with the pecans. May store the cake, covered, in the refrigerator for up to 3 weeks before serving. Flavor improves over time. Yield: 15 servings.

CREAM CHEESE FROSTING

8 ounces cream cheese, softened
$1/4$ cup margarine, softened
1 teaspoon vanilla extract
2 cups confectioners' sugar

Combine the cream cheese and margarine in a mixing bowl and beat until well blended. Add the vanilla and confectioners' sugar and beat until of spreading consistency.

Approx Per Serving: Cal 372; Prot 4 g; Carbo 64 g; T Fat 12 g; 28% Calories from Fat;
Chol 45 mg; Fiber 1 g; Sod 335 mg

UPSIDE-DOWN PEACH SPICE CAKE

3 tablespoons butter
$^1/_4$ cup packed brown sugar
1 (29-ounce) can sliced peaches, drained
$^1/_2$ cup melted butter
$^1/_2$ cup sugar   1 egg
$2^1/_2$ cups sifted flour
$1^1/_2$ teaspoons baking soda
$1^1/_2$ teaspoons cinnamon
1 teaspoon ginger $^1/_2$ teaspoon nutmeg
$^1/_2$ teaspoon cloves
$^1/_2$ teaspoon salt
$^1/_2$ cup molasses $^1/_2$ cup honey
1 cup hot water

Melt 3 tablespoons butter in a 9×9-inch baking pan. Sprinkle the brown sugar evenly over the melted butter. Arrange the peach slices in a decorative pattern in the pan, cutting large peach slices if necessary. Set the prepared pan aside. Combine $^1/_2$ cup melted butter, sugar and egg in a large bowl and beat until well blended. Combine the flour, baking soda, cinnamon, ginger, nutmeg, cloves and salt in a medium bowl and mix well.

Blend the molasses, honey and hot water in a small bowl. Add the flour mixture and molasses mixture to the sugar mixture alternately, mixing well after each addition. Spoon the batter carefully over the peaches.

Bake at 350 degrees for 45 to 50 minutes or until the cake tests done. Loosen the cake from the sides of the pan and invert onto a heatproof tray. Lift the pan carefully. Use a spatula to replace any peach slices on the cake. Serve warm with whipped cream or ice cream. Yield: 9 servings.

Approx Per Serving: Cal 459; Prot 5 g; Carbo 80 g; T Fat 15 g; 29% Calories from Fat;
Chol 62 mg; Fiber 2 g; Sod 504 mg

RHUBARB SOUR CREAM CAKE

1/4 cup butter, softened
1 1/2 cups packed brown sugar
1 egg
1 tablespoon vanilla extract
2 to 3 cups flour
1 teaspoon salt
1 teaspoon baking soda
1 cup sour cream
4 cups (1/2-inch pieces) red rhubarb
1/2 cup sugar
1/2 teaspoon nutmeg

Cream the butter and brown sugar in a mixing bowl until light and fluffy. Add the egg and vanilla and beat until blended. Sift the flour, salt and baking soda together. Add enough of the flour mixture to the creamed mixture to make the batter of the desired consistency, mixing well. Fold in the sour cream and rhubarb. Spoon into a greased and floured 9×13-inch cake pan. Mix the sugar and nutmeg together and sprinkle over the batter. Bake at 350 degrees for 40 minutes or until the cake tests done. Yield: 12 servings.

Approx Per Serving: Cal 342; Prot 5 g; Carbo 62 g; T Fat 9 g; 22% Calories from Fat;
Chol 37 mg; Fiber 2 g; Sod 366 mg

 4/18/1896—Rhubarb is plentiful and happy we are that it is, for since mince meat has left market there has been a crying after a good pie. Pies filled with preserves of any kind are not the tempting morsel a rhubarb or green apple pie is.

—Morning Republican

RUM CAKE

1 (2-layer) package yellow cake mix
1 (4-ounce) package vanilla instant pudding mix
4 eggs
1/2 cup water
1/4 cup vegetable oil
1/2 cup dark rum
Rum Glaze

Combine the cake mix, pudding mix, eggs, water, oil and rum in a large mixing bowl. Beat with an electric mixer at medium speed for 4 minutes. Pour the batter into greased and floured tube pan. Bake at 325 degrees for 1 hour. Cool in the pan for 15 minutes. Invert onto a cake plate.

Prick the hot cake all over with a cake tester or skewer. Spoon the warm Rum Glaze over the warm cake slowly and carefully to allow the glaze to soak into the cake. May sprinkle chopped nuts over the bottom of the cake pan before adding the batter. Yield: 16 servings.

RUM GLAZE

1 cup sugar
1/2 cup margarine
1/4 cup water
1/2 cup dark rum

Combine the sugar, margarine, water and rum in a saucepan. Heat until the sugar dissolves, stirring constantly. Bring to a boil and boil for 5 minutes.

Approx Per Serving: Cal 344; Prot 3 g; Carbo 44 g; T Fat 14 g; 37% Calories from Fat;
Chol 54 mg; Fiber <1 g; Sod 387 mg

SHOOFLY CAKE

3 cups flour   1 cup sugar
$^1/_2$ cup butter
1 cup water   1 cup mild molasses
1 teaspoon baking soda

Combine the flour and sugar in a bowl and mix well. Cut in the butter until crumbly; reserve 1$^1/_2$ cups of the mixture for topping. Bring the water to a boil in a large saucepan. Stir in the molasses. Remove from the heat and stir in the baking soda. Add the remaining flour mixture to the molasses mixture and mix well with a wire whisk. Pour into a greased and floured 8×12-inch cake pan. Sprinkle the reserved mixture over the top. Bake at 350 degrees for 30 minutes. Yield: 12 servings.

Approx Per Serving: Cal 319; Prot 3 g; Carbo 59 g; T Fat 8 g; 22% Calories from Fat;
Chol 21 mg; Fiber 1 g; Sod 194 mg

 COMING FULL CIRCLE IN CHESTER COUNTY

In 1993 I began a family research project for a friend of mine and in the process I found out about my family also. I didn't know much about my ancestors beyond a few vague details about my great grandparents but I know about all of them now.

May Landis Marion was my paternal grandmother. Our ancestors, Philip and Catharine, came to Butler County, Ohio, from Tredyffrin/Easttown Township, in 1816. Descendents of theirs still live in the Landis homestead near Trenton, Ohio. I am the last member of my family's branch to have been born in Butler Country, Ohio, but I haven't lived there for a long time.

In 1773 our forefather Frederick and his wife Elizabeth raised their family next to the Revolutionary war hero General "Mad" Anthony Wayne. In 1777 the Landis family was within earshot of the "Battle of Paoli" and the encampment at Valley Forge, and their tract of land is just three miles from my home of today.

I found out that I travel the same roads as my family once did, and I have come full circle from my birthplace in Butler County, Ohio, to the birthplace of my ancestors in Paoli located in Chester County, Pennsylvania.

—*Susanna Marion Baum*

GULIELMA PENN LE FEVRE'S
WAR CAKE (1925)

2 cups packed brown sugar
2 cups raisins
2 cups water
1 tablespoon cinnamon
1 teaspoon cloves
$1/2$ teaspoon salt
2 tablespoons shortening
3 cups flour
2 teaspoons baking soda

Combine the brown sugar, raisins, water, cinnamon, cloves, salt and shortening in a large saucepan. Bring to a boil, stirring until the brown sugar dissolves completely. Boil for 5 minutes. Let stand until cool.

Sift the flour and baking soda together. Add to the raisin mixture and mix well. Pour into greased and floured 9×13-inch cake pan. Bake at 350 degrees for 1 hour or until the cake tests done. Yield: 15 servings.

Approx Per Serving: Cal 276; Prot 3 g; Carbo 63 g; T Fat 2 g; 7% Calories from Fat; Chol 0 mg; Fiber 2 g; Sod 260 mg

 Indian Hannah died in 1802, aged 72, the last of the Lenapes to live in Chester County.

Cakes

ONE-TWO-THREE-FOUR CAKE

1 cup butter, softened
2 cups sugar
4 egg yolks
2^2/$_3$ cups flour
1^1/$_2$ teaspoons baking powder
^{1}/$_2$ teaspoon salt
1 to 1^1/$_2$ cups sour cream
4 egg whites
1^1/$_2$ teaspoons vanilla extract

Beat the butter in a mixing bowl until fluffy. Add the sugar gradually, beating until light and fluffy. Add the egg yolks and beat until well blended. Sift the flour, baking powder and salt together. Add to the creamed mixture alternately with the sour cream, beating well after each addition but do not overbeat. Beat the egg whites until stiff peaks form. Fold the vanilla extract and stiffly beaten egg whites into the batter gently.

Pour the batter into 2 greased and floured 9-inch round cake pans. Bake at 350 degrees for 30 to 35 minutes or until the cakes test done. Cool in the pans for about 15 minutes. Remove to wire racks to cool completely. Frost as desired. Yield: 10 servings.

Approx Per Serving: Cal 544; Prot 7 g; Carbo 67 g; T Fat 28 g; 46% Calories from Fat;
Chol 150 mg; Fiber 1 g; Sod 421 mg

BUCKEYES

1 cup margarine
1^1/2 cups graham cracker crumbs
^{1}/2 cup chopped pecans
1 cup shredded coconut
1 (1-pound) package confectioners' sugar
1 tablespoon vanilla extract
1 (12-ounce) jar peanut butter
1 cup semisweet chocolate chips
1 to 2 tablespoons finely chopped paraffin

Melt the margarine in a large saucepan over low heat. Remove from the heat and add the graham cracker crumbs, pecans, coconut, confectioners' sugar and vanilla and mix well. Add the peanut butter and mix until the mixture can be handled. Shape the mixture into small balls and place on waxed paper. Combine the chocolate chips and paraffin in a double boiler over hot water. Heat until the chocolate and paraffin melt and blend well. Dip the peanut butter balls into the chocolate to coat and place on waxed paper. Let stand until the chocolate coating is firm. Yield: 60 buckeyes.

Approx Per Buckeye: Cal 131; Prot 2 g; Carbo 14 g; T Fat 8 g; 54% Calories from Fat;
Chol 0 mg; Fiber 1 g; Sod 85 mg

12/26/1889—Christmas, 1889 will go on record as the warmest one ever experienced in West Chester. The streets were dusty and bicyclists appeared in their summer costumes. Overcoats were laid aside and summer clothing was brought into use.

—*Daily Local News*

CHERRY SQUARES

1 cup flour
3 tablespoons confectioners' sugar
^{1}/2 cup butter, softened
2 eggs
1 teaspoon vanilla extract
1 cup sugar
^{1}/4 cup flour
^{1}/2 teaspoon baking powder
^{1}/4 teaspoon salt
^{3}/4 cup chopped pecans
^{1}/2 cup shredded coconut
^{1}/2 cup quartered drained maraschino cherries

Combine 1 cup flour and confectioners' sugar in a mixing bowl and mix well. Add the butter and mix with fingers until the mixture is smooth and well mixed. Press evenly into an ungreased 8×8-inch baking pan. Bake at 350 degrees for 20 minutes or until golden brown.

Beat the eggs in a mixing bowl. Add the vanilla and sugar and mix well. Combine ^{1}/4 cup flour, baking powder and salt in a bowl and mix well. Add to the egg mixture and mix well. Stir in the pecans, coconut and maraschino cherries. Spread the mixture evenly over the baked layer. Bake for 25 minutes longer. Let stand until cool. Cut into squares. Yield: 16 squares.

Approx Per Square: Cal 209; Prot 2 g; Carbo 26 g; T Fat 11 g; 47% Calories from Fat;
Chol 42 mg; Fiber 1 g; Sod 126 mg

CHOCOLATE NUT DREAMS

1 (2-layer) package chocolate cake mix
$^1/_3$ cup evaporated milk
$^3/_4$ cup melted butter
1 cup chopped pecans
60 vanilla caramels
$^1/_2$ cup evaporated milk
1 cup semisweet chocolate chips

Combine the cake mix, $^1/_3$ cup evaporated milk and butter in a bowl and mix well. Add the pecans and mix well. Press half the mixture evenly over the bottom of a greased 9×13-inch baking dish. Bake at 350 degrees for 8 minutes. Place the caramels in the top of a double boiler over simmering water. Add $^1/_2$ cup evaporated milk and cook until the caramels are melted and the mixture is smooth and well blended. Spoon the caramel mixture over the baked cake layer. Sprinkle with the chocolate chips and additional pecans if desired. Top with the remaining cake mix mixture. Bake for 18 minutes longer. Cool completely before cutting into bars. Yield: 16 servings.

Approx Per Serving: Cal 478; Prot 6 g; Carbo 62 g; T Fat 26 g; 46% Calories from Fat; Chol 28 mg; Fiber 2 g; Sod 465 mg

 The people who make constant use of chocolate are the ones who enjoy the most steady health and are the least subject to a multitude of little ailments which destroy the comfort of life; their plumpness is also more equal. (1908, *Choice Recipes*)

CHOCOLATE CHIP SQUARES

1 cup butter, softened
$1/2$ cup sugar
$1/2$ cup packed brown sugar
3 egg yolks
1 tablespoon water
2 cups flour
$1/8$ teaspoon salt
2 cups semisweet chocolate chips
1 cup chopped pecans
3 or 4 egg whites
1 cup packed brown sugar

Cream the butter, sugar and $1/2$ cup brown sugar in a mixing bowl until light and fluffy. Beat the egg yolks with water. Add the beaten egg yolks to the creamed mixture and mix well. Mix the flour and salt together. Add to the creamed mixture and mix until smooth. Spread the mixture over the bottom and up the sides of a greased 10×15-inch shallow baking pan. Sprinkle with the chocolate chips and pecans.

Beat the egg whites in a mixing bowl at high speed until soft peaks form. Add 1 cup brown sugar gradually, beating constantly until stiff peaks form. Spread the meringue over the chocolate chips and pecans, sealing to the edge. Bake at 350 degrees for 30 to 35 minutes or until light brown. Let stand until cool. Cut into squares. My mother always made these squares for Easter.
Yield: 60 squares.

Approx Per Square: Cal 107; Prot 1 g; Carbo 14 g; T Fat 6 g; 46% Calories from Fat;
Chol 19 mg; Fiber 1 g; Sod 43 mg

DATE BARS

10 to 14 ounces pitted dates
$^{1}/_{2}$ cup sugar
$^{1}/_{2}$ cup water
$1^{1}/_{2}$ cups flour
1 teaspoon baking powder
$1^{1}/_{2}$ cups rolled oats
1 cup packed brown sugar
$^{3}/_{4}$ cup melted butter

Cut the dates into small pieces and place in a saucepan. Add the sugar and water and mix well. Cook over medium heat until a thick paste forms, stirring frequently. Set aside to cool. Combine the flour, baking powder, oats and brown sugar in a large bowl. Add the melted butter and mix well. Press half the oats mixture into a 9×9-inch baking pan. Spread the date mixture evenly in the prepared pan. Press the remaining oats mixture evenly over the dates. Bake at 375 degrees for 35 to 40 minutes or until light brown. Let stand until cool. Cut into bars. Yield: 16 bars.

Approx Per Bar: Cal 292; Prot 3 g; Carbo 52 g; T Fat 9 g; 28% Calories from Fat;
Chol 23 mg; Fiber 3 g; Sod 125 mg

 1/17/1889—It is estimated that nearly 5 tons of candy were eaten in West Chester and vicinity during the holiday season just closed . . . Prices ranged from $12^{1}/_{2}$ cents to $1 per pound. Most of the candy came from Philadelphia and the manufacturers are said not to use the highly poisonous substances in coloring that are so freely used in making cheap candy.

—*Daily Local News*

FRUITCAKE COOKIES

2 pounds candied cherries
1 pound seedless raisins
6 cups pecan halves
4 cups flour
1 teaspoon baking soda
1 teaspoon cinnamon
1 teaspoon allspice
1 teaspoon cloves
1 teaspoon nutmeg
$1/2$ cup butter, softened
$1^1/2$ cups packed brown sugar
4 eggs
1 cup whiskey or orange juice

Cut the candied cherries into halves and combine with the raisins and pecans in a bowl. Add $1/2$ cup of the flour, mix until coated and set aside. Sift the remaining $3^1/2$ cups flour, baking soda, cinnamon, allspice, cloves and nutmeg together and set aside. Cream the butter and brown sugar in a large mixing bowl until light and fluffy. Add the eggs 1 at a time, beating well after each addition. Add the sifted dry ingredients alternately with the whiskey, mixing well after each addition. Add the candied cherry mixture and mix well.

Drop by teaspoonfuls onto a greased cookie sheet. Bake at 300 degrees for 15 minutes. Cool on the cookie sheet for 1 to 2 minutes and remove to wire racks to cool completely.
Yield: 150 cookies.

Approx Per Cookie: Cal 90; Prot 1 g; Carbo 13 g; T Fat 4 g; 36% Calories from Fat;
Chol 7 mg; Fiber 1 g; Sod 18 mg

OLD-FASHIONED GINGERSNAPS

2 cups flour
1 tablespoon baking soda
$^1/_2$ teaspoon salt
1 teaspoon cloves
1 teaspoon ginger
1 teaspoon cinnamon
$^3/_4$ cup butter, softened
1 cup sugar
1 egg, slightly beaten
$^1/_4$ cup molasses
$^1/_2$ cup (or more) sugar

Sift the flour, baking soda, salt, cloves, ginger and cinnamon together and set aside. Cream the butter and 1 cup sugar in a large mixing bowl until light and fluffy. Add the egg and molasses and mix well. Add the sifted dry ingredients and mix well. Shape the dough into 1-inch balls and roll in $^1/_2$ cup sugar, adding additional sugar if needed. Arrange on a lightly greased cookie sheet.

Bake at 350 degrees for 8 to 10 minutes or until light brown. Cool on the cookie sheet for 1 to 2 minutes and remove to wire racks to cool completely. Yield: 60 cookies.

Approx Per Cookie: Cal 60; Prot 1 g; Carbo 9 g; T Fat 2 g; 36% Calories from Fat;
Chol 10 mg; Fiber <1 g; Sod 107 mg

JAN HAGELS

1 cup butter, softened
1 cup packed brown sugar
1 egg yolk
1 teaspoon vanilla extract
2 cups flour
$1/8$ teaspoon salt
1 egg white, slightly beaten
$1/4$ cup sugar
$1/2$ teaspoon cinnamon
$1/2$ cup sliced unblanched almonds

Cream the butter and brown sugar in a mixing bowl until light and fluffy. Add the egg yolk and vanilla and mix until well blended. Mix the flour and salt together. Add to the creamed mixture and mix well.

Pat the mixture into an ungreased 12×18-inch baking pan. Brush with the beaten egg white. Mix the $1/4$ cup sugar and cinnamon together. Sprinkle the cinnamon-sugar and almonds over the top.

Bake at 350 degrees for 15 minutes. Cut into bars while warm. Yield: 100 bars.

Approx Per Bar: Cal 39; Prot <1 g; Carbo 5 g; T Fat 2 g; 49% Calories from Fat;
Chol 7 mg; Fiber <1 g; Sod 23 mg

 On June 2, 1715, David Lloyd sold to John Cadwalader 250 acres of land in Uwchland for 75 pounds.

MINCE DOODS

6 cups flour
$^1/_2$ teaspoon salt
$^3/_4$ cup water
2 cups (heaping) shortening
1 (9-ounce) jar mincemeat

Mix the flour and salt in a large bowl. Measure 1 cup of the mixture and transfer to a small bowl. Add the water to the small bowl, mixing to form a smooth paste and set aside. Cut the shortening into the remaining flour mixture until crumbly. Add the flour paste and mix with a fork until the mixture clings together. Divide the pastry into 4 portions and shape into balls. Roll 1 portion at a time on a lightly floured surface and cut with a 3-inch cutter.

Place a heaping teaspoon of the mincemeat on half the pastry rounds. Moisten the edges with water and top with the remaining rounds, pressing to seal and making a decorative edge with a fork. Arrange on an ungreased cookie sheet. Bake at 400 degrees for 15 minutes or until golden brown. Cool on the cookie sheet for 1 to 2 minutes and remove to wire racks to cool completely. This is a Pennsylvania German family recipe. Yield: 36 cookies.

Approx Per Cookie: Cal 187; Prot 2 g; Carbo 18 g; T Fat 12 g; 57% Calories from Fat; Chol <1 mg; Fiber 1 g; Sod 39 mg

5/15/1897—Gossip about the meats is useless. Every buyer has a sense of judgment which tells him what is seasonable; and as for prices, well, the butcher is getting rich off you, and there is no remedy.

—*Morning Republican*

GRANDMOTHER BRENNER'S
GERMAN SUGAR COOKIES

1 cup butter, softened
1 cup shortening
1^1/2 cups packed brown sugar
4 eggs
2 egg yolks
6 to 6^1/2 cups flour
^{1}/2 teaspoon salt
1 teaspoon cinnamon
1 teaspoon baking powder
^{1}/2 cup milk
^{3}/4 cup brandy
^{1}/2 cup finely chopped pecans
2 egg whites, slightly beaten
1 cup (about) confectioners' sugar

Cream the butter, shortening and brown sugar in a large mixing bowl until light and fluffy. Add the eggs and egg yolks and beat until well blended. Mix 6 cups of the flour, salt and cinnamon together and set aside. Dissolve the baking powder in the milk and add the brandy. Add the flour mixture to the creamed mixture alternately with the milk mixture, mixing well after each addition. Add enough additional flour to make dough of the desired consistency. Add the pecans and mix well. The dough will be soft. Chill, covered, for 2 hours or longer or until the dough is firm enough to handle.

Roll the dough very thin on a lightly floured surface. Cut with cookie cutters and arrange on well greased cookie sheets. Brush the cookies with the beaten egg whites and sprinkle with confectioners' sugar. Bake at 425 degrees for 6 to 10 minutes or until light golden brown; do not overbake. Cool on the cookie sheets for 1 to 2 minutes and remove to wire racks to cool completely. Yield: 100 cookies.

Approx Per Cookie: Cal 126; Prot 2 g; Carbo 18 g; T Fat 5 g; 36% Calories from Fat;
Chol 18 mg; Fiber <1 g; Sod 43 mg

*VINEGAR COOKIES

1 cup butter, softened
3/4 cup sugar
1 teaspoon vanilla extract
2 teaspoons vinegar
1 teaspoon baking soda
1³/4 cups flour
1 cup raisins (optional)

Cream the butter and sugar in a mixing bowl until light and fluffy. Add the vanilla, vinegar and baking soda and blend well. Add the flour and mix well. Stir in the raisins. Drop by teaspoonfuls onto a lightly greased cookie sheet.

Bake at 325 degrees for 12 to 15 minutes or until light brown. Cool on the cookie sheet for 1 to 2 minutes and remove to wire racks to cool completely.

These cookies were served by Mrs. Ellis Stern of Coatesville to the volunteers when they visited her home to see her majolica collection in the late 1970s. Yield: 36 cookies.

Approx Per Cookie: Cal 96; Prot 1 g; Carbo 12 g; T Fat 5 g; 48% Calories from Fat;
Chol 14 mg; Fiber <1 g; Sod 88 mg

 In 1702 Richard Baker paid Peter Bezellin one pound, four shillings for one dozen "Tommy-hawks."

NORTHBROOK ORCHARDS' DUTCH APPLE CRUMB PIE

3 or 4 large baking apples, peeled, sliced
1 unbaked (9-inch) pie shell
$1/2$ cup sugar
2 tablespoons flour
1 teaspoon cinnamon
$1/4$ teaspoon nutmeg
$1/2$ cup sugar
$1/2$ cup flour
$1/2$ cup butter, softened
$1/2$ cup chopped pecans

Arrange the apple slices in the pie shell. Combine $1/2$ cup sugar, 2 tablespoons flour, cinnamon and nutmeg in a small bowl and mix well. Sprinkle over the apples.

Combine $1/2$ cup sugar and $1/2$ cup flour in a small bowl and mix well. Cut in the butter until the mixture is crumbly. Mix in the pecans. Sprinkle the pecan mixture over the top.

Bake at 350 degrees for 1 hour or until the apples are tender and the topping is brown.
Yield: 8 servings.

Approx Per Serving: Cal 443; Prot 3 g; Carbo 56 g; T Fat 24 g; 48% Calories from Fat;
Chol 31 mg; Fiber 3 g; Sod 235 mg

HEARTSTONE ORCHARD APPLE PIE

7 to 8 cups thinly sliced peeled apples
1/4 to 1/2 cup sugar
2 tablespoons flour
1 teaspoon cinnamon
3/4 teaspoon freshly ground nutmeg
1/8 teaspoon salt
1 tablespoon lemon juice
Cold Water Pastry

Use a variety of apples for the filling such as Jonathan, Granny Smith, Baldwin and Cortland in any combination and proportion. Place the apple slices in a large bowl. Combine the sugar, flour, cinnamon, nutmeg and salt in a small bowl and mix well. Sprinkle over the apples. Add the lemon juice and toss to mix.

Divide the Cold Water Pastry into 2 portions. Roll 1 portion on a lightly floured surface and fit into a 9 1/2-inch deep-dish pie plate. Spoon the apple mixture into the pastry-lined pie plate. Roll the remaining pastry to fit over the top, sealing and fluting the edge and cutting vents. Bake at 425 degrees for 45 minutes or until golden brown. Yield: 8 servings.

COLD WATER PASTRY

3/4 cup butter
1 egg
2 tablespoons cold water
1 3/4 cups unbleached flour

Combine the butter, egg and water in a food processor. Pulse 6 times to mix well. Add the flour and pulse until the mixture forms a ball. Place the dough in a sealable plastic bag, squeeze out the air and seal tightly. Knead the dough in the bag and shape into a disc. Chill in the refrigerator for 2 hours or longer.

Approx Per Serving: Cal 380; Prot 4 g; Carbo 51 g; T Fat 19 g; 43% Calories from Fat;
Chol 73 mg; Fiber 3 g; Sod 221 mg

*WHITE VELVET CHEESECAKE PIE

9 ounces cream cheese, softened
1/2 cup sugar
2 eggs, beaten
1/2 teaspoon vanilla extract
Graham Cracker Pie Shell
2 cups sour cream
1/2 teaspoon vanilla extract
5 tablespoons sugar
1/8 teaspoon cinnamon

Beat the cream cheese in a mixing bowl until light. Add 1/2 cup sugar gradually, beating until light and fluffy. Beat in the eggs and 1/2 teaspoon vanilla. Pour into the Graham Cracker Pie Shell. Bake at 325 degrees for 20 minutes or until firm. Blend the sour cream, 1/2 teaspoon vanilla, 5 tablespoons sugar and cinnamon in a bowl and pour over the cream cheese layer. Bake for 5 minutes longer. Let stand until cool. Chill until serving time. Yield: 8 servings.

GRAHAM CRACKER PIE SHELL

1 1/3 cups fine graham cracker crumbs
1/4 cup melted butter

Combine the graham cracker crumbs and butter in a bowl and mix with hands until the mixture holds together. Press the crumb mixture evenly over the bottom and side of a 9-inch pie plate. Bake at 350 degrees for 5 minutes and set aside.

Approx Per Serving: Cal 467; Prot 7 g; Carbo 39 g; T Fat 32 g; 61% Calories from Fat;
Chol 129 mg; Fiber 1 g; Sod 321 mg

NANTUCKET PIE

2 cups fresh cranberries
$1/2$ cup chopped walnuts
$1/2$ cup sugar
2 eggs
1 cup sugar
1 teaspoon almond extract
$3/4$ cup melted butter
1 cup flour

Rinse the cranberries and pat dry. Place the cranberries in a well greased 9- or 10-inch pie plate. Add the walnuts and sprinkle $1/2$ cup sugar over the top. Beat the eggs in a mixing bowl. Add 1 cup sugar, almond extract and butter and beat until smooth. Add the flour and beat until smooth; the mixture will be thin. Pour over the layers.

Bake at 375 degrees for 35 to 40 minutes or until golden brown and a wooden pick inserted in the center comes out clean; do not overbake. Cut into wedges and invert the wedges onto dessert plates. Serve warm or cold with vanilla ice cream or whipped topping or as a breakfast cake. Yield: 6 servings.

Approx Per Serving: Cal 577; Prot 6 g; Carbo 72 g; T Fat 31 g; 47% Calories from Fat; Chol 133 mg; Fiber 2 g; Sod 258 mg

*CHOCOLATE PIZZA

$3/4$ cup corn syrup
$1/3$ cup heavy cream
8 ounces semisweet chocolate
$1/2$ cup butter
$2/3$ cup sugar
2 eggs
1 teaspoon vanilla extract
$3/4$ cup flour
$1/2$ teaspoon salt

Combine the corn syrup and cream in a medium heavy saucepan over medium heat. Bring to a boil, stirring occasionally. Break the chocolate into pieces and add to the hot mixture. Heat until the chocolate melts, stirring constantly; reserve $2/3$ cup of the chocolate sauce.

Add the butter and sugar to the remaining sauce in the saucepan and stir until the butter melts and the sugar dissolves completely. Remove from the heat. Beat the eggs in a bowl. Stir a small amount of the hot mixture into the eggs; stir the eggs into the hot mixture. Blend in the vanilla. Mix the flour and salt together. Stir into the chocolate mixture gradually. Spread the mixture evenly in a greased pizza pan.

Bake at 350 degrees for 20 minutes or until firm. Cool in the pan for 10 minutes. Remove to a wire rack to cool completely. Top with ice cream, fruit and nuts as desired and drizzle the reserved chocolate sauce over the top or may sprinkle with grated white chocolate and drizzle with hot fudge sauce.

This recipe originated with Michael Pillagalli and appeared in *Early American Life,* December 1991, with photos of his house at Christmas. Yield: 12 servings.

Approx Per Serving: Cal 322; Prot 4 g; Carbo 42 g; T Fat 19 g; 48% Calories from Fat;
Chol 65 mg; Fiber 1 g; Sod 214 mg

KEY LIME PIE

Pace One Restaurant

7 egg yolks
1 cup lime juice
1 tablespoon grated lime rind
2$^1/_2$ (14-ounce) cans sweetened condensed milk
Graham Cracker Crust

Beat the egg yolks in a mixing bowl until thick and lemon-colored. Add the lime juice and rind and mix well. Add the sweetened condensed milk and blend well. Pour into the Graham Cracker Crust. Bake at 325 degrees for 25 to 30 minutes or until firm. Let stand until cool. Serve with whipped cream. Store the pie in the refrigerator. Yield: 10 servings.

GRAHAM CRACKER CRUST

2 cups graham cracker crumbs
2 tablespoons sugar
$^1/_4$ cup melted butter

Mix the graham cracker crumbs and sugar in a bowl. Add the melted butter and mix well. Press over the bottom and side of a 10-inch pie plate. Bake at 325 degrees for 8 minutes. Let stand until cool.

Approx Per Serving: Cal 519; Prot 12 g; Carbo 77 g; T Fat 19 g; 33% Calories from Fat; Chol 195 mg; Fiber 1 g; Sod 323 mg

SHAKER LEMON PIE

2 lemons, thinly sliced
2 cups sugar
4 eggs
Several drops of lemon extract
1 recipe (2-crust) pie pastry

Combine the lemon slices and sugar in a bowl and mix well. Let stand for several hours. Beat the eggs with lemon extract, add to the lemon slices and mix well. Divide the pastry into 2 portions. Roll 1 portion on a lightly floured surface and fit into a pie plate. Spoon the lemon mixture into the pastry-lined pie plate. Roll the remaining pastry to fit over the top, sealing and fluting the edge and cutting vents.

Bake at 450 degrees for 15 minutes. Reduce the oven temperature to 350 degrees. Bake for 30 minutes longer or until a knife inserted in the center comes out clean. Yield: 8 servings.

Approx Per Serving: Cal 462; Prot 6 g; Carbo 72 g; T Fat 17 g; 33% Calories from Fat;
Chol 106 mg; Fiber 2 g; Sod 266 mg

 In 1742 Benjamin Franklin experimented with his newly invented stove in a fireplace in what is now Coventry Hall, the office of the French & Pickering Creeks Conservation Trust.

SOUTHERN PECAN PIE

3 eggs
3/4 cup sugar
1/2 teaspoon salt
1 cup light corn syrup
1 tablespoon melted butter
1 teaspoon vanilla extract
1 cup pecan halves
1 unbaked (9-inch) pie shell

Beat the eggs in a bowl just until well mixed. Add the sugar, salt, corn syrup, butter and vanilla and mix until well blended. Place the pecans in the pie shell. Pour the egg mixture over the pecans.

Place the pie in a preheated 400-degree oven and reduce the temperature to 350 degrees immediately. Bake for 40 to 50 minutes or until firm. Let stand until cool. Serve with whipped cream. Yield: 8 servings.

Approx Per Serving: Cal 433; Prot 5 g; Carbo 63 g; T Fat 20 g; 40% Calories from Fat; Chol 84 mg; Fiber 2 g; Sod 350 mg

SWEET POTATO PIE

2 cups mashed cooked sweet potatoes
2 tablespoons butter, softened
2 eggs
1 cup sugar
1 tablespoon flour
$1/2$ teaspoon salt
$1/4$ teaspoon baking soda
$1/2$ cup buttermilk
1 teaspoon vanilla extract
1 unbaked (9-inch) pie shell

Combine the mashed sweet potatoes, butter and eggs in a mixing bowl and mix well. Combine the sugar, flour and salt in a medium bowl and mix well. Add to the sweet potato mixture and mix well.

Dissolve the baking soda in the buttermilk and stir into the sweet potato mixture. Blend in the vanilla. Pour into the pie shell. Bake at 350 degrees for 1 hour and 10 minutes or until set. Serve warm or cooled. Yield: 8 servings.

Approx Per Serving: Cal 350; Prot 5 g; Carbo 57 g; T Fat 12 g; 30% Calories from Fat;
Chol 61 mg; Fiber 2 g; Sod 374 mg

 Circa 1862—RECEIPT FOR RHEUMATISM

1 pint of rye whiskey
$1/4$ pound of stone brimstone (pulverized)

Take $1/2$ gill of it 3 mornings in succession. Stir well before taking.

—*Anna B. Temple*

A "FINE OLD INN..."

Taverns were a familiar and welcome sight in 18th-century Chester County. The first ones had been established in the late 17th century along old Indian trails as settlers first came into what was then known as William Penn's Welsh Tract. By the early 18th century, wagon routes had been established on which more traffic appeared. Demand for food and lodging continued to increase, and by the middle of the 18th century, farm ownership began to boom.

The Turk's Head Inn was established in 1761 by Phineas Eachus. Located in what was then known as Goshen, the tavern offered all manner of liquor and food and lodging, the rates for which were posted according to the laws of Pennsylvania's charter. Eachus sold his tavern to John Hoopes, who expanded it and advertised it as a "more commodious house for the accommodation of travelers where lodgings, food, cider, punch and other liquor can be obtained." The borough of West Chester began to grow up around the Turk's Head, and by the early 1800s, the tavern was an important social center and meeting place.

Not all taverns enjoyed as fine a reputation as the Turk's Head. The Blue Bell Inn near Paoli was run by a three-time widow, whose hospitality was less than sterling. The Blue Bell had a reputation for mediocre food and even worse lodging. In September of 1778, Christopher Marshall of Philadelphia wrote of his stay at the Blue Bell: it "had little to offer the sensitive palate." His meal consisted of "salt pork and turnip tops, along with a heavy sour bread." Sleeping accommodations were worse; Marshall had to share a bed with a stranger and, "for fear of fleas and bugs," slept in his coat and stockings.

During the period preceding the Revolution, taverns became important meeting places for political debate among the local county residents. The Revolution itself saw many taverns, such as the Bull Tavern near Phoenixville, frequented by members of both the British and American military, including General Howe, Benedict Arnold, and George Washington. Some, however, met their demise during the Revolution; the Inn at Yellow Springs was abandoned, and the British ransacked the Dilworthtown Inn and turned it into a prison.

Tavern ownership again flourished in 1794 when the construction of the Lancaster Turnpike made travel between Philadelphia and Lancaster a common occurrence. The sixty-six-mile route boasted sixty-seven taverns, including the popular Ship Inn near Exton, owned by John Bowen and his wife. Known for its delicious food, such as "hot brandied mince pies and potent coffee," clean bedding, and jovial atmosphere, the Ship Inn demonstrated a hospitality that is still so prevalent today among Chester County inns and taverns.

George Washington referred to the Bull Tavern near Phoenixville as a "fine old inn."

Volunteer Appreciation Luncheon

Shrimp Pita Wedges
(PAGE 26)

Cheese Biscuits
(PAGE 128)

Curried Walnuts
(PAGE 29)

Chinese Chicken Salad
(PAGE 49)

Mesclun Greens with Summer Dressing
(PAGE 51)

Cool Carrot and Pineapple Salad
(PAGE 48)

Lady Chocolate Mousse
(PAGE 181)

Twinings Black Currant Tea Iced or Green Tea and Spice

HEALTHY APPLE CRISPY

4 large cooking apples.
1 teaspoon cinnamon
1 teaspoon nutmeg
$1/4$ cup butter, softened
$1/4$ cup packed light brown sugar
$1/2$ cup flour
$1/2$ cup rolled oats

Peel the apples and slice thinly. Arrange the apple slices in a lightly greased 2-quart baking dish. Sprinkle with cinnamon and nutmeg and toss lightly. Cream the butter and brown sugar in a mixing bowl until light and fluffy. Add the flour and oats and mix until crumbly. Sprinkle over the apples. Bake at 375 degrees for 30 to 45 minutes or until the apples are very tender. Serve with vanilla ice cream or whipped topping. Yield: 4 servings.

Approx Per Serving: Cal 340; Prot 4 g; Carbo 56 g; T Fat 13 g; 33% Calories from Fat;
Chol 31 mg; Fiber 5 g; Sod 123 mg

*From *Anna B. Temple: Her Diaries,* published by the Uwchland Township Historical Commission in 1990. Susannah W. Brody and Constance T. Happersett, eds. Found in the CCHS library. Anna was born in 1845, lived in Lionville, and was a Quaker. Her father was a tanner. Anna attended school at Ercildoun Seminary. (*A.B.T.)

12/12/1863—Wet all day. This evening we were entertained by the skill of some of the girls in making a "Cabbage Chicken" and dutch Dolly as they sewed them. I laughed so much at them. After that Miss Nellie played the piano for us. *A.B.T.

APPLE RING TAPIOCA

^{1}/4 cup quick-cooking tapioca
^{1}/2 cup packed brown sugar
^{1}/2 teaspoon salt
^{1}/2 teaspoon mace
^{1}/2 teaspoon cinnamon
2 teaspoons lemon juice
1 teaspoon grated lemon zest
2 cups water
2 tart red apples
3 tablespoons brown sugar
1 tablespoon butter, softened

Combine the tapioca, ^{1}/2 cup brown sugar, salt, spices, lemon juice, lemon zest and water in a saucepan. Bring to a boil over medium heat, stirring constantly. Remove from the heat. Core the apples and cut each apple into 4 to 6 rings. Arrange half the rings in a greased baking dish. Spoon the tapioca mixture over the apple rings, covering completely. Mix the 3 tablespoons brown sugar with 1 tablespoon butter and spread over the remaining apple rings. Arrange the apple rings brown sugar side up over the tapioca mixture. Bake at 400 degrees for 30 minutes or until the apples are tender. Serve warm. May serve with cream or ice cream. Yield: 4 servings.

Approx Per Serving: Cal 223; Prot <1 g; Carbo 51 g; T Fat 3 g; 12% Calories from Fat;
Chol 8 mg; Fiber 2 g; Sod 335 mg

12/25/1863—. . . Again our hearts have been made glad by the joyous Christmas. Many families have been called together to dine under the parental roof around the happy board, but many, *very* many, are not seen at the family table that enlivened the brothers and sisters but one short year ago. Some are in the Camp far among the pine trees of the South, while some lie in the silent grave beneath the damp clods of the valley, exempt from the cares of the world, no more to hear the merry shouts of "Christmas gift" ring through the halls of home. John, Ella & H.M. went down to her father's to spend Christmas, eat roast turkey. Mother and I spent the afternoon in Lionville. We took tea at Aunt Lydia Lee's. . . . *A.B.T.

EASY NO-CRACK CHEESECAKE

16 ounces reduced-fat cream cheese, softened
$^3/_4$ cup sugar   2 eggs, beaten
1 teaspoon vanilla extract
1 cup reduced-fat sour cream
1$^1/_3$ cups zwieback crumbs
$^1/_4$ cup sugar
$^1/_4$ cup melted butter

Combine the cream cheese and $^3/_4$ cup sugar in a mixing bowl and beat until light and fluffy. Add the eggs and vanilla and beat until smooth. Blend in the sour cream. Combine the zwieback crumbs and $^1/_4$ cup sugar in a bowl and mix well. Add the melted butter and mix well. Press the crumb mixture over the bottom and side of a 10-inch pie plate. Spoon the cream cheese mixture into the crust. Bake at 350 degrees for 30 to 35 minutes or until firm. Let stand until cool. Refrigerate until serving time. Yield: 8 servings.

Approx Per Serving: Cal 397; Prot 11 g; Carbo 42 g; T Fat 21 g; 47% Calories from Fat;
Chol 110 mg; Fiber 0 g; Sod 298 mg

1/9/1864—. . . This evening we had a Pantoscopic exhibition. Some magnificent photographs were thrown upon canvas by means of the Drummond light. It represented them more brilliantly than any thing of that kind has ever done. They consisted of residences of the distinguished, such as W. Irving's at Sunny Side, Washington's at Mt. Vernon, and many other statuary. Scenes for Niagara, one where Mr. Irvin's wife and child were standing. I recognized him immediately. I think two of the most beautiful of all were an old Abbey by moonlight. We could see half of the moon, the stars shining, it was sublime; and a vessel on the ocean, rocking to and fro, a lighthouse was seen at the right. We enjoyed them all very much, quite a large audience was present. *A.B.T.

1/11/1864—. . . A gentleman came down in a large two horse sleigh—the horses were loaded with bells—this evening to take all the girls or as many as could get in. But neither Lizzie nor Richard were at home, and Miss Nellie could not give us permission. The gentleman had to go away without any school girls. So much for that. *A.B.T.

CREAM CUSTARD CRUMB TORTE

5 tablespoons flour $^1/_2$ cup cold milk
2 cups milk $^3/_4$ cup sugar
2 egg yolks, beaten
1 teaspoon vanilla extract
Zwieback Crust
2 egg whites   2 tablespoons sugar
$^3/_4$ cup zwieback crumbs $^1/_4$ cup sugar
1 teaspoon cinnamon
$^1/_4$ cup melted butter

Combine the flour and $^1/_2$ cup cold milk in a small bowl, mix until smooth and set aside. Place 2 cups milk in the top of a double boiler and heat until the milk scalds. Stir the flour mixture into the hot milk. Add $^3/_4$ cup sugar and stir until the sugar dissolves completely. Stir a small amount of the hot mixture into the beaten eggs; stir the eggs into the hot mixture. Cook until the mixture is thickened and smooth, stirring frequently. Blend in the vanilla. Pour the mixture into the Zwieback Crust. Beat the egg whites in a mixing bowl until soft peaks form. Add 2 tablespoons sugar gradually, beating constantly until stiff peaks form. Spread the meringue over the custard, sealing to the edge. Combine the zwieback crumbs, $^1/_4$ cup sugar, cinnamon and butter in a bowl and mix well. Sprinkle over the meringue. Bake at 300 degrees for 25 minutes or until golden brown. Serve with whipped cream. Yield: 8 servings.

ZWIEBACK CRUST

$^3/_4$ cup zwieback crumbs
$^1/_4$ cup sugar
1 teaspoon cinnamon
$^1/_4$ cup melted butter

Combine the zwieback crumbs, sugar and cinnamon in a medium bowl and mix well. Add the butter and mix well. Press the crumb mixture over the bottom of a 7×11-inch shallow baking dish. Bake at 325 degrees for 10 minutes.

Approx Per Serving: Cal 386; Prot 6 g; Carbo 53 g; T Fat 17 g; 39% Calories from Fat; Chol 95 mg; Fiber <1 g; Sod 211 mg

*LADY CHOCOLATE MOUSSE

2 large packages ladyfingers
8 ounces German's sweet chocolate
3 tablespoons water
3 cups whipping cream
1 teaspoon vanilla extract
2 tablespoons confectioners' sugar
4 egg whites
4 egg yolks
3 tablespoons sugar

Line the bottom and side of a springform pan with ladyfingers. Chop the chocolate and combine with the water in the top of a double boiler over hot water. Heat until the chocolate melts, stirring frequently and set aside. Combine the whipping cream, vanilla and confectioners' sugar in a bowl. Whip the whipping cream until soft peaks form. Beat the egg whites in a medium bowl until stiff peaks form and set aside. Beat the egg yolks with the sugar in a large mixing bowl until thick and lemon-colored. Add the melted chocolate gradually, beating constantly until smooth. Fold in the stiffly beaten egg whites gently. Fold in about 2/3 of the whipped cream gently. Spoon the mixture into the prepared springform pan. Top with the remaining whipped cream. Freeze for 1 1/2 hours before serving. Garnish with choice of toppings such as chocolate shavings, strawberries or raspberries. Yield: 8 servings.

Approx Per Serving: Cal 680; Prot 11 g; Carbo 59 g; T Fat 47 g; 60% Calories from Fat;
Chol 405 mg; Fiber 1 g; Sod 121 mg

 2/20/1864—Very nice day, warmer. We had school until 9 1/2 a.m. Some of the girls went to gather evergreens to trim the stage. . . . I spent all evening in the music room listening to the notes of the piano, Smith's March my favorite. Annie Jones played for me. Fannie Bowman sang the "Gypsy girl," which is indeed beautiful. I will ever think of her when I hear it sung. . . . *A.B.T.

2/23/1864—. . . This evening after supper, some of us went out and enjoyed ourselves by playing "Drop the handkerchief" and we had a gay time. We returned to the house and began making flowers again. *A.B.T.

SOUL-SOOTHING BREAD PUDDING

1 (16-ounce) loaf Italian or French bread
3 Granny Smith apples
1 cup dried cranberries
$3/4$ cup sugar
6 eggs
2 cups milk
2 cups light cream
$1^1/2$ teaspoons vanilla extract

Cut the bread into thin slices. Core the apples and cut into slices. Alternate layers of bread slices, apples slices, cranberries and sugar in a buttered 8- or 9-inch square baking dish $1/3$ at a time until all the ingredients are used, ending with bread slices. Sprinkle with a small amount of additional sugar. Beat the eggs in a large mixing bowl. Add the milk, cream and vanilla and beat until combined. Pour the mixture over the layers. Bake at 350 degrees for 1 hour or until a knife inserted in the center comes out clean. Serve warm with vanilla ice cream or custard sauce.
Yield: 8 servings.

Approx Per Serving: Cal 562; Prot 13 g; Carbo 69 g; T Fat 26 g; 42% Calories from Fat; Chol 234 mg; Fiber 4 g; Sod 429 mg

2/24/1864—. . . We had no school today, trimming the schoolroom, etc., occupied the former part of the day. After dinner, Edith Davis curled my hair. . . . At 7 p.m., the curtain was drawn. . . . One colloquy, entitled "The Priestess' Gift Altar," was beautiful. I was Priestess, standing behind an altar. Annie Jones, (Spring) came first, dressed in white trimmed with green, brought her basket of green. A. Hughes (Summer), dressed in white brought her gift, a basket of roses . . . . Next, the Goddess of Liberty in white with red, white and blue roses, with a large flag. *A.B.T.

9/21/1864—I received an invitation to "A leap year party" or "Basket sociable" to be held in Isaac Lewis' barn, the ladies are to defray all expenses. *A.B.T.

GREAT-GRANDMOTHER HANNUM'S CHERRY PUDDING

3 1/2 cups flour
1/2 teaspoon salt
2 teaspoons baking powder
3 eggs
2 cups milk
1 tablespoon melted butter
2 cups seeded sour cherries
Hard Sauce

Combine the flour, salt and baking powder in a large bowl and mix well. Beat the eggs in a medium mixing bowl. Add the milk to the eggs and mix well. Add the egg mixture and butter to the flour mixture and beat until smooth. Stir in the cherries. Pour into a greased double boiler. Cook, covered, over simmering water for 3 hours. Serve warm with Hard Sauce. Yield: 8 servings.

HARD SAUCE

1/4 cup butter, softened
1 cup confectioners' sugar
1 teaspoon vanilla extract
2 egg whites

Cream the butter, confectioners' sugar and vanilla in a mixing bowl until light and fluffy. Beat the egg whites in a bowl until stiff peaks form. Add the egg whites to the creamed mixture and mix until smooth. Place the sauce on ice to thicken and harden.

Approx Per Serving: Cal 411; Prot 11 g; Carbo 65 g; T Fat 12 g; 26% Calories from Fat;
Chol 107 mg; Fiber 2 g; Sod 410 mg

*GINGERBREAD PUDDING

3 cups crumbled stale gingerbread
3 tablespoons minced crystallized ginger
2 eggs
1/3 cup packed brown sugar
2 cups apple juice
1 teaspoon vanilla extract
1 cup chopped pecans

Sprinkle the gingerbread crumbs on a baking sheet. Heat in a 350-degree oven for 20 minutes or until crisp and toasted. Place the crumbs in a loaf pan and sprinkle with the ginger. Beat the eggs in a mixing bowl. Add the brown sugar and beat until blended. Whisk in the apple juice and vanilla. Pour the mixture over the crumbs and let stand for 10 minutes. Sprinkle the pecans over the top. Bake at 350 degrees for 50 minutes or until a knife inserted in the center comes out clean. Serve sliced or scooped from the pan and garnished with a sprinkle of confectioners' sugar or whipped cream. May be served warm or cold. Yield: 6 servings.

Approx Per Serving: Cal 346; Prot 5 g; Carbo 42 g; T Fat 19 g; 48% Calories from Fat; Chol 79 mg; Fiber 2 g; Sod 113 mg

1/2/1865—John, Hannah, Mary and I went to a party at P. Vickers' this evening, there were 50 there. I danced like a "trooper," it is splendid. I have got a basket of the delicious fruit and I long for more. I enjoyed myself very much, we had cake and apples. I heard the lovely notes of the piano, Emmie played for me. We got home at 12 M. *A.B.T.

Note: *The allegorical reference to partaking of the fruit of forbidden pleasure in third sentence.*

4/7/1865—John went to Lionville this evening. There was quite an excitement among its inhabitants. All the houses were illuminated. The men marched around accompanied with drums, bells, old kettles, etc., making quite a noise, and long after the hour of midnight could be heard in a distance the dunning of cannon, the ringing of bells, etc., in honor of the great victory, the fall of Richmond . . . . *A.B.T.

EASY ENGLISH TRIFLE

1 (2-layer) package yellow cake mix
1/4 cup (or less) brandy or cognac
2 (4-ounce) packages vanilla pudding mix
4 cups milk
4 or 5 bananas, sliced
1 (10-ounce) package frozen strawberries, thawed
1 (10-ounce) package frozen raspberries, thawed, drained
1/2 cup whipping cream, whipped

Prepare and bake the cake mix in round layer cake pans according to the package directions. Split the layers into thin layers if desired. Select a deep trifle bowl that is narrower at the bottom than at the top if possible. Trim the cake layers in varying diameters in order to fit the smaller layers at the bottom of the bowl and the larger layers near the top. Sprinkle each cake layer with a small amount of the brandy. Prepare the pudding mixes with the milk according to the package directions.

Alternate layers of cake, pudding, bananas, partially drained strawberries and raspberries in the bowl until all the ingredients are used or to about 1/2 inch from the top of the bowl. Cover with whipped cream. Garnish with chocolate curls. Refrigerate for several hours or overnight before serving. Yield: 12 servings.

Approx Per Serving: Cal 387; Prot 5 g; Carbo 65 g; T Fat 12 g; 27% Calories from Fat;
Chol 26 mg; Fiber 2 g; Sod 569 mg

9/5/1865—Beautiful day, cool. John, Hannah M., Mary and I went to the Celebration at Lionville. Three schools met, they had a brass band, it was grand. I was with Em Vickers and her Cousin Mary Webster some time, I enjoyed myself finely. *A.B.T.

Contributors

Susan H. Aggarwol
Lorraine S. Armstrong
Joyce Aspen
Nancy L. Bailey
Stacey H. Ballard
Lois H. Bassett
Susan Marion Baum
Sandra L. Beale
Elizabeth T. Beck
Elizabeth M. Bell
Suzanne Betts
Constance Bond
Gloria W. Boyer
Carole Bradley
Judith L. Bradley
Claudie J. Brock
Susannah W. Brody
Edward C. Broge
Joan P. Broge
Jane S. Brosius
Karen Brosius
Sharon L. Brown
Jane Buffam
Amy L. Cacchio
Gilbert F. Cardnell
Amy Cassio
Catherine Christensen
Teresa T. Ciccotelli
Elizabeth Clark
Harriette M. Clark
Ruth H. Collins
Anne M. Congdon
Mimi Connelly
Barbara R. Copeland
Phyllis M. Copeland
Virginia Cordes
Catherine S. Cottell
Irene Crichton
David N. Daddezio

Elizabeth Daley
Nancy C. D'Angelo
Daughters of the British
    Empire/Lady Churchill
    Chapter
Doris W. Davis
Jane B. Davis
Pamela K. Davis
Allison Dea
Gay S. Denny
Marilyn A. Dietz
Mary W. Dowd
Kathy G. Duggan
Linda-Lee Egen
Ellen E. Endslow
Jean J. Evans
Jill Evans
Emedio Falini
Dottie L. Fehr
Lucia N. Ferrero
Judith Finnigant
Elizabeth A. Fisher
Barbara M. Fry
Melissa D. Fry
Roberta H. Garbisch
Kathleen Garrett
Carol Ware Gates
Karin E. Gedge
Elizabeth U. Gilpin
Andrea T. Glidden
George R. Graham Jr.
George R. Graham III
Sally N. Graham
Carol K. Grigson
Roger Grigson
Nancy Halladay
Mildred C. Haller
Elizabeth B. Halsted
Antonia W. Hamilton

Cindy Harris
Joy B. Hartshorn
Christine Hasen
Elanie Heist
Doris B. Hemker
Lauretta Colesworthy
    Hickman
Mary C. Hickman
Mrs. Walter Scott Hill
Vivien H. Hoare
Deborah B. Hodies
Barbara L. Holcroft
Myrtle Hollingsworth
Anna Hood
Brenda J. Hoopes
Varney T. Hoopes
Jean E. Hoover
Janc Ann Hornberger
Marilyn S. Horne
Beverley S. Hotton
Marilyn Reich Hovey
Lynne Y. Hoyt
Susan B. Hudson
Lynn S. Huff
Gussie A. Irons
Corlet W. Jackson
Elsie S. John
Faith C. Johnson
Joan S. Johnston
Sandy H. Kalemjian
Ann G. Kampf
Ella Marie Kean
D. J. Keen
Barbara B. Kidder
Claire R. Kocik
Suzanne Krishna
Miriam O. LePatourel
Marilyn J. LeFevre
Christine F. Leinberger

Contributors

Dorothy Lindsey
Mary Jane Littlepage
Nancy C. Lukens
Charles R. A. Lyddane
Helen B. Lynch
Susan A. MacDonnell
Andy J. Manidis
Sandy A. Manthorpe
Wendy M. Manthorpe
Dorothy Martelli
Karen L. Martynick
Tracy Massey
Mary Elizabeth McClellan
Charlene J. McGowan
Ida C. McIntyre
Mary Ann McNeff
Susan M. McSherry
Maureen B. Menseck
Michael B. Mento
Jaylene Miller
Kitty L. Miller
Marge Miller
Nancy L. Mohr
Patricia P. Mooberry
Edna McNeil Moore
Hulduh J. B. Moss
Sandy Mull
Charlotte M. Nickerson
Northbrook Orchards
Marilyn P. Nulty
A. Bonnie O'Donnell
Susan E. O'Donnell
Helen E. Olseski
Vickey Ormsby
Margaret Woodward Ostrom
Elise J. Payne
Marian E. Peterson
Mary Louise Phillips
Marge Pickett

Nancy G. Pike
Michael A. Pillagalli
Mary E. Pomeroy
Elizabeth LeP. Powell
Alexandra B. Powers
Bea D. Quaintance
Ruth J. Rainer
Jean W. Raleigh
Anna M. Reckenwald
Suzanne T. Richard
Jane F. Richards
Marjorie B. Ricker
Deb C. Ridgeway
Carolee K. Risk
Mary E. G. Robinson
Nancy D. Rogal
Judith M. Rosato
Barbara J. Rutz
Carol L. Samuelson
Dawn L. Samuelson
Dr. Mark Saracino
Margaret P. Sarmento
Francey Scafario
Susan P. Schultz
Margaret H. Sharp
Julia W. Smedley
Peggy Smith
Heather A. Snyder
Serita Spadoni
Special Teas Tea Room
Barbara Spellman
Mrs. Ellis Stern
Alexandra P. Stetzer
Diane Stevens
Howard Stevens
Jacqueline P. Stine
Phyllis J. Stively
Elizabeth Stoltzfus
Marie Elena R. Stotler

Betsy A. Struck
Ann Sullivan
Jane Swisher
Steffi S. Swope
Miriam R. Taylor
Thelma L. Temple
Bob Thompson
Carol N. Thompson
Nancy Thompson
Trish Tolomeo
Susan D. Topp
Mary Anne Toto
Virginia Hamilton Trexler
Theo Turner
Viki Turner
Barbara J. Tuttle
Elizabeth B. Twaddell
Sam H. G. Twining, L.V.O.,
    O.B.E.
Elaine G. Vincent
Elizabeth Wagoner
Michael J. Walters
Clara Edwards Ware
Ruth F. Weeks
Rosemary Weiss
The Western Reserve
    Herb Society
Anne B. Wiegle
Mary C. Williams
Hope Middleton Wood
Renny Wood
William S. Wood II
Isabelle H. Woodrow
Roland H. Woodward
Lee Yetter
Jean R. Yoder
Ginny Ziegler

Index

To Order More Cookbooks . . .

THE CHESTER COUNTY HISTORICAL SOCIETY

225 North High Street, West Chester, Pennsylvania 19380-2691
Attention: Cookbook
Telephone: (610) 692-4800 Fax: (610) 692-4357
Website: www.chestercohistorical.org

Name

Street Address

City   State   Zip

Telephone (   )

Your Order	Qty	Total
Delectable Collectables at $19.95 per book		$
Postage and handling at $3.00 per book		$
Pennsylvania residents add 6% sales tax		$
Total		$

Method of Payment: [   ] VISA   [   ] MasterCard

[   ] Check payable to CCHS — Cookbook

Account Number   Expiration Date

Signature

Cases of 6, 12 or 24 millennium cookbooks are available at a discount. Dealers encouraged.
Call **The Chester County Historical Society** at (610) 692-4800.

~ This form may be photocopied. ~

Join Us Now. We're on the Move.

THE CHESTER COUNTY HISTORICAL SOCIETY

225 North High Street, West Chester, Pennsylvania 19380-2691
Telephone: (610) 692-4800 Fax: (610) 692-4357
Website: www.chestercohistorical.org

Name(s)
_____

Street Address
_____

City _____ State _____ Zip _____

Home Telephone (   )_____ Office Telephone (   )_____

I/We wish to join at the following level:

[   ] Individual Senior Citizen $ 25
[   ] Individual $ 30
[   ] Family $ 40
[   ] Contributor $ 100
[   ] Patron $ 250
[   ] Associate $ 500
[   ] Benefactor $1,000

Method of Payment:

[   ] VISA
[   ] MasterCard
[   ] Check payable to CCHS

Account Number
_____   Expiration Date

Cardholder Name
_____   Amount Charged $

Signature
_____

Gift Memberships: Call CCHS at (610) 692-4800

[   ] *Please send me information about volunteer opportunities.*

~ This form may be photocopied. ~